NOTES ON THE FAMINE TOUR BY HIS HIGHNESS THE MAHARAJA GAEKWAR

NOTES ON THE FAMINE TOUR BY HIS HIGHNESS THE MAHARAJA GAEKWAR

Sayaji Rao Gaekwar

GYAN

Published by

GYAN

Gyan Publishing House
5, Ansari Road
Daryaganj, New Delhi-110002
Phone: 011-47034999, 9811692060
E-mail: books@gyanbooks.com

Distribution Network
gyanbooks.com
India, USA, Canada, UK, Australia, France

ISBN : 978-81-212-9464-5 (PB)
First Published, 1901

2nd Impression 2023

Printed at: Gyan Press, Delhi.

NOTES ON THE FAMINE TOUR BY HIS HIGHNESS THE MAHARAJA GAEKWAR

Author: Sayaji Rao Gaekwar

NOTES ON THE FAMINE TOUR

LABOURERS AT WORK [Frontispiece.

NOTES ON THE FAMINE TOUR BY HIS HIGHNESS THE MAHARAJA GAEKWAR

PRIVATELY PRINTED

1901

CONTENTS

I.—KADI DIVISION

FAMINE TOUR

II.—AMRELI DIVISION

CONTENTS

FAMINE TOUR

III.—BARODA CITY AND DIVISION

CONTENTS

DABHOI

IV.—NAVSARI DIVISION

FAMINE TOUR

APPENDIX

LIST OF ILLUSTRATIONS

KADI DIVISION

I.—KADI DIVISION

1. As soon as the Famine administration had been well settled and relief-works had been opened in order to mitigate the distress of the people, I thought of visiting my northern dominions, where the cry of distress had been heard at a comparatively early date. Kadi Division. 4th Dec. to 11th Dec. 1899.

2. I visited Mehsana, Vadnagar, Patan, Kalol, and Kadi, as well as the villages situated in the vicinity of these towns, and acquainted myself with the sufferings of their inhabitants and their expectation of relief from the State. The village people were very simple, and it was a pleasure to converse with these good-hearted, honest folk, whose unsophisticated minds left a favourable impression on me. It had never before given me greater pleasure to converse with the people in their own language, and to be able to move among them, often without their knowing who I was. I frequently try to mix with the people in this way, and, as frequently, I discover in the communion a source of interest and of instruction to myself. The guileless children of the soil, when simply and sympathetically questioned, poured forth their unvarnished tales of pleasure and of pain, of jealousy and of scandal. They reckoned up the Places visited during the tour.

out-turn of their crops, and the heavy demand made on their income by the savkar. They told me of the way in which they helped their blind or infirm neighbours, their professional beggars as well as those who, through some mischance, had been reduced to mendicancy. But when an inkling of the rank of their questioner began to dawn upon them, as they noticed the number of armed followers present, they would very naturally begin to make their little personal request for remission and for more tagavi, demands which would form a most useful base of inquiry and scrutiny after one's return from such riding excursions.

Codification of famine rules.

3. As soon as the signs of famine became dimly apparent in the latter part of August, I applied myself to the study of the famine rules which lay hidden among the State records; and after their perusal I set myself to work to amplify and codify them, with the assistance of some of my officers. I gave special attention to the question of organisation, as the rules touching this matter were either altogether wanting, or were startlingly deficient. It is the very point in which the executive, and emphatically our executive, has to be strengthened by the clearness of the instructions imparted. Apart from this, I had my own ideas regarding some of the matters dealt with in the famine code; but as I was pressed for want of time, owing to the rapidity with which the famine was assuming a more and more threatening aspect, I had to postpone any attempt to introduce my ideas into the rules. I gave certain orders, however, which were really

meant to test the value of some of the plans that had suggested themselves to me. Later, and as soon as I had had the opportunity of coming into closer contact with the relief-works, I set myself to collect information and statistics with a view to see if I could gather sufficient material for the success of my general plan. I tried to collect this information on some of the works in a way which might serve to illustrate my views, and I now leave it to speak for itself. The information, though meagre in quantity and quality, had to be extracted under considerable pressure both from the sufferers and from those who had been sent to assist them, and in some places special machinery and a special agency had to be applied to obtain it. The official world is slow to move, and is slower still to imbibe new ideas. I have, later on, drawn up a regular form of the information which almost every labourer is expected to bring with him filled up by his village Patel. Apart from my desire to solve certain general problems, I consider it essential to know the condition and status of the men we have to deal with on famine relief-works. In this, as well as in many matters, I am aware that I can create a spirit of inquiry by initiating measures, but their proper execution must depend upon the willingness and energy of others. What the ultimate success of my schemes may be will be discovered only some time after the famine has passed away.

4. I issued orders that tagavi advances of amounts not exceeding thirty rupees might be granted for the maintenance of people who had neither a holding nor property of any other

Tagavi for maintenance.

kind, but who were withheld by sentiment from resorting to the relief-works. This tagavi for maintenance was advanced to the recipient without any collateral guarantee.

Tagavi to Ekankadi and Fartaankadi village-holders.

5. The condition of the people living in villages held on the Ekankadi and Fartaankadi tenures also attracted my early attention. The Matadars of these villages had scarcely the means to maintain themselves, absolutely none to support the poor agriculturalists in their villages who had been thrown out of employment in this season of general distress. Orders were passed during my tour sanctioning the expenditure of one lakh of rupees on tagavi for the maintenance of landholders in the villages of the two abovementioned classes.

Tagavi to coppersmiths at Visnagar.

6. During my visit to Visnagar I was told that the coppersmiths of that town were actually starving for want of any demand for the produce of their labour. Visnagar in normal years is a busy mart for the copper-trade, and its artisans make a fair profit. Copper, however, had lately, owing to several circumstances, greatly risen in price, and the famine had had its usual depressing effect on the trade conditions of the country. The artisans had consequently been thrown out of employment and were reduced to a pitiable plight. Orders were given to set apart a sum of 2000 rupees to be spent in tagavi advances to the smiths. Sentiment had prevented them from resorting to the relief-works, and they were only too glad to avail themselves of the relief thus provided.

Private charity in Kadi.

7. I was much gratified at observing the extent to which private charity was exerting

itself to mitigate the effects of the famine. In every large town a poorhouse had been opened where numbers of maimed and crippled destitutes were being fed and lodged. In Patan two poorhouses were being entertained on a grand scale, and others have sprung up since. Visnagar also possessed a decent poorhouse managed by private enterprise. The Subha of Kadi deserves credit for having evoked such philanthropic sentiments in the minds of the wealthy citizens of his division, for their noble charity could not have secured better objects for help and support than the emaciated sufferers of Kadi. The resources of Government are not unbounded, and the ways in which Government has to mete out relief are many. If private charity supplements the work of Government, the latter has more scope to utilise its resources in ways which must perforce baffle private enterprise. The Subha, as well as his private coadjutors, has deserved well of his country by fostering institutions for the relief of the poor, the infirm, the aged, and the decrepit. They have maintained the good name Gujarat has always proudly enjoyed, of being a land where charity abounds.

Gyarmi and Sadavarat institutions utilised for relief purposes.

8. Though private charity was thus in a measure able to take care of the poor and the helpless in large towns, the same generous aid could not always be extended to small out-of-the-way villages. There we could not look for the humane support of the wealthy, and Government stepped in where private charity slackened or was found wholly wanting. The moment had not then come to open poorhouses broadcast over the country. That might have had a demoralising

influence, one tending to foster habits of indolence and to produce a want of self-reliance. Besides, the burden on the State would scarcely have been bearable. With a view to avoid too lavish an expenditure at a very early stage, and yet to secure the objects of relieving the wants of the helpless and the infirm, other measures were adopted. In every Mahal some grants from the State are provided from which Sadhus and Fakirs are feasted on stated days and occasions. These Gyarmi and Sadavarat institutions, though quite in consonance with the old and cherished ideals of our Native States, may not be deemed quite deserving of retention in a season of widespread distress and suffering. The indiscriminate charity bestowed on institutions which support a crowd of tricky and lazy ascetics could not be regarded as a fit form for State charity, so long as such a truly bitter appeal for help came to us from other quarters. The Vahivatdars of Pattan and other talukas were accordingly instructed gradually to stint the rations served out to the Fakirs and the Jogis, and to employ the saving thus effected in relieving famine-stricken people who had not strength enough to work on the relief-works.

Grants to prevent death by starvation.

9. The Vahivatdars and higher revenue officials were directed to be constantly on the move and to inspect village after village in order to see that no helpless or destitute person was neglected and left to die. Subhas were invested with discretionary powers to make grants up to 100 rupees, and Vahivatdars up to 50 rupees, to individuals in want of help. These grants were renewable when exhausted. The district

officers were thus enabled to help the really needy and to prevent the occurrence of deaths from starvation.

10. The Peta Mahal of Harij, even in times of prosperity, is proverbially poor, and has for its population a class of cultivators who live from hand to mouth and can ill afford to lay by wealth for times of adversity. The land, the great natural agency of agricultural wealth, is poor and apt to turn saltish; nor is there any fresh subsoil water which can be utilised for irrigation, so that the Peta Mahal has always to depend upon the fall of the monsoon. In such a tract it is not difficult to conceive that the cry of distress was very great, and it was not an act of folly on the part of the inhabitants to quit their homes and homesteads in quest of "fresh fields and pastures new." From the reports received regarding the prevailing distress and from specimens of Harij inhabitants observed on the Gangadi tank, it was thought desirable to give them early relief. The Minister and the Sar Subha very praiseworthily undertook to visit this Mahal and to see for themselves what was the condition of its people.

Dispensation of gratuitous relief at Harij.

11. Most of all, among the helpless and destitute, did the little children inspire me with the greatest compassion. Their famished and miserable appearance and their plaintive cries in the streets had from an early date made a most painful impression on me. An orphanage was ordered to be opened and located at some central and convenient spot, where all deserted children and orphans below the age of twelve could be comfortably housed, fed, and trained up.

Orphanage of Mehsana.

Becharaji was first suggested as a suitable spot for such an orphanage, but afterwards Mehsana was selected as a more accessible centre for the Kadi division, and the Subha was instructed to collect all unclaimed children and orphans and to maintain them in the institution. Since then another State orphanage has been opened at Baroda for the Baroda division, and instructions were issued to harbour in it some 200 orphans. In Baroda, too, private charity has been instrumental in founding a second institution for orphans, where about 300 young children are maintained under the supervision of a private committee.

Lying-in arrangements at the hospitals for destitute women.

12. The other objects of special pity and solicitude were women who had either just been confined or were about to be confined. There were instances in which such women had to work on the relief-works when on the eve of their travail. Orders were issued to grant accommodation and assistance to all child-bearing women who could obtain no other assistance. The hospitals and dispensaries of the State were thrown open to them for a certain period of time before and after their confinement. It is gratifying to see from the monthly returns that a number of these destitute women are taking advantage of the provision made for them.

Relief-works.

13. After having thus met the needs of the helpless and the destitute, my attention was directed to the relief-works in the Kadi division, and I made it my object to discover what they were, how they were managed, and what good they were effecting.

14. There were about sixty relief-works

going on in the Kadi district in December, which employed a daily average of about 16,000 labourers. Most of them were of purely local interest, having been opened too near the homes of the necessitous rayats. Some not only completely set at naught the principle of the distance test, but were unscrupulously monopolised by the people of the village within whose boundaries they had been opened. The inhabitants successfully prevented people of other villages from resorting to their works, either by actual threats or by a display of unfriendly feeling. The officials who looked after these works seldom bestirred themselves to inquire into and set right the selfish action of the Mewasi relief-seekers. The Huzur officials, either owing to coercion from certain quarters, or under a gush of feeling (shall I say of misplaced philanthropy?), or from a desire to make up for previous shortcomings, rushed hurriedly into ill-considered enterprises, and started fresh works, though they possessed no knowledge of the country and had not consulted local officials. The local officials, who got rid of the trouble of minute supervision by appealing to the orders which came to them direct from the Huzur, attempted to account for their own shortcomings by advancing the old plea that they feared the "omnipotent" Huzur officers. They too deserve censure, but we may now afford to forgive and forget these petty bickerings, at any rate in instances where the result has not been positively injurious to the rayats or costly to the State. Too near the homes of the rayats.

15. In consequence of the mistakes made, great multitudes of people were attracted to the Their large number.

works; and as the distress was then only at an initial stage, the numbers of the relief-seekers gave no sure indication of the degree of distress prevailing in the district.

I must further note that most of the works, whether proposed or actually in operation at this date, consisted of tanks or small roads of no definite utility. The Public Works and other Departments had been dilatory in preparing relief programmes, and in submitting large useful projects to the consideration of Government; and the consequence was that these minor works were the only means of support the labourers could fall back upon.

What followed?

In view of the unsettled state of the programme of relief-works and the fact that the proximity of works to villages afforded too easy an admission of labourers, I directed some of the minor works to be closed, so as to bring the entire number of them down to between thirty and forty.

Reduction of works.

16. I trusted that the following advantages would accrue to us from the reductions if the order was properly carried out:—

(*a*) A saving would take place in the labour of supervision, with a proportionate increase of efficiency.

(*b*) The distance test would give us a true indication of the degree of distress, and would exclude any element of recklessly lavish, and therefore mischievous, expenditure. It was advisable that only those labourers who were really pinched should elect to go to the works, and the end would be obtained by placing these at a distance from the homes of the relief-seekers.

(*c*) The mere tinkering at tanks which

admitted of considerable enlargement would be avoided by starting a few works at a time and by finishing them to the utmost. It was a mistake to take up a multitude of works, only to leave them in a state of incompleteness and proportionate uselessness.

17. At the time I was on tour, the Kadi programme contained only two or three works of any magnitude, viz.: the Vijapur-Kalol railway and the Vadnagar feeder. But if these were started early in the season there were legitimate grounds for anticipating a dearth of useful projects at a later date. The distress might by that time have become far more serious and the urgency of the need for relief might be really pressing. Similar fears had been realised in the Amreli division. To avoid the danger, and after taking into consideration the number of large works at my disposal, I was forced to indicate such dates for the starting of major works as would leave a provision for the more advanced stages of the distress. The liberality of Government in furnishing relief-works should, I felt, develop as the distress grew keener. Since then some large schemes have been prepared and sanctioned for the Kadi division. Had these schemes been matured and kept ready earlier in the day, Nature of these works.

(1) The wastage on minor works of doubtful utility would have been avoided;

(2) Large works of real value would have been started and completed;

(3) The distance test would have enabled us from the beginning to gauge the real distress in Kadi; and

(4) A large number of useful minor schemes could have been held over till the monsoon, when work may advantageously be brought to the very door of the rayat.

Gangadi tank, task system.

18. Relief-works were opened at Harij and Patan at a comparatively late date, and after the distress in the western part of the division had become widespread and acute. The consequence was that the inhabitants were worn out at too early a date. It followed, too, that when the Gangadi tank was opened at Patan, some of the labourers were found incapable of turning out the work imposed on them by the code. The officers in charge then erred in another way, by keeping on the work without imposing or exacting any task at all. Thereupon large numbers of labourers flocked to the Gangadi tank, some of whom were really incapable, while others, capable enough, were simply attracted to the spot by the prospect of earning easy wages at a comparatively small cost to themselves. The sums originally allotted to the scheme were soon exhausted; repeated sanctions were asked for and granted; and, eventually, the work turned out was very small when compared with the expenditure.

Imposition of tasks and classification of labourers.

19. The officers of the Public Works Department complained bitterly of this "no task system," wrongly styled by them and the Subha as "the daily payment system." It was certainly not a mode of relief contemplated by the code. The Gangadi tank quickly became a regular hive of local drones, and its fame as a place where applicants for work were admitted without difficulty and wages paid for nothing

spread so rapidly, that people resorted to this spot in preference to works that were going on in the vicinity of their own villages. This implies that the natives, though disinclined to go far in search of a livelihood, are ready enough to push to a distance if they find that they will be supported for doing nothing or next to nothing. In the same way they would be ready to migrate if they found the authorities determined to give them work at a distance only.

There are times when we have to enforce the principle of a fair *quid pro quo.* Obstinacy has to be cured by a counterbalancing display of obstinacy. On the Gangadi work the weak and the strong were indiscriminately huddled together, and all were made to work without the imposition of any definite task. When my attention was drawn to this evil, I ordered the labourers to be classed separately: (1) one class was to comprise those who were really capable of working; and (2) a second was to consist of people who were out of condition.

Tasks were ordered to be imposed on the first class, and work was to be exacted from them in return for the money spent. Greater attention was ordered to be paid to the code.

20. With regard to the second class, it was ordered that those who were ill and suffering from any infirmity should be removed to a special famine hospital at Patan. Those who only required nursing to be restored to their former condition were to be employed on a separate block of work, where light work was to be exacted from them, without any set task. Second class of labourers.

At Patan the work of excavating the ruins of the old city was assigned to this second class, with a view to possibly bringing to light the remains of the ancient city of Anhilvada. Why should we not, in our humble way, follow the example set us by archæologists in the better-known cities of Egypt, Greece, Italy, and Palestine?

Complaints made to me by labourers.

21. I must bear in mind that I am writing down my personal impressions, so again I return to a description of my method of inspection.

Before visiting Patan I had seen labourers at work in Mehsana, Vadnagar, and Visnagar, and of course in the city of Baroda. It was my wont to visit these people during my stay at their work once or oftener, to mark their physical condition, and listen to their grievances, to make inquiries of them regarding the amount and punctuality of the payments of their wages, and to ascertain whether they were in any way wrongly dealt with. Beside this, I frequently rode into villages attended by a few followers, and sometimes quite alone, riding across what should have been fields and cultivated land. I was thus able to converse with passers-by, men, women, and children, without being recognised by them. I elicited from them most useful information on various points, and learnt the ways and means by which they hoped to meet the exceptional season. It was personal observation which enabled me to grasp the extent of physical deterioration in the huge number of labourers plying their work with the humming noise of busy bees on the lofty banks of the Gangadi tank. Some there were who thought

NEW ADMISSIONS IN THE VISNAGAR ANNAGRUHA

[*Face page 7.*

the work a useless undertaking, while others considered it a piece of pure wisdom ; but all were unanimous in believing that it was a benevolent undertaking on the part of Government, started and carried out to afford the means of subsistence to famine sufferers. The physical condition of some of the labourers did certainly strike me as worse than anything I had seen elsewhere, except in the capital, for nowhere else had I met people so emaciated.

But next to Baroda, the condition of the Gangadi folk was the most distressing I had witnessed, and, as I have said, the wretchedness of those among them who came from Harij was, even here, conspicuous. I grant, however, that I had to be on my guard against some exaggeration in the description given to me of the misery of those who had swarmed in from Harij. To find out the exact truth I had to take into consideration the previous unhealthy state of the Harij population before I could make up my mind as to the extent of the suffering actually wrought by the famine. I do not, however, think there can be any divergence of opinion on one point : when we did assist the Harij folk, we did not do so a moment too soon. They really required more food and less work. In the course of all my tours and visits to different Talukas I was never more unpleasantly impressed than by the sight of the poorhouses of Patan, and of the old and emaciated men at work at Gangadi. My pity was as deep only when, at a later date, I looked on the forlorn and despairing countenances of the Kodinar people, so hard hit by the great scourge, and again, though to a slighter degree, when I passed among the people of unhealthy Khambha.

Shortcomings of officers.

22. Throughout my tours I have noticed that, except for an intelligent but small minority, the employées, and particularly those of the Public Works Department on whom really fell the execution of the relief policy, were strangers, at times to an astonishing degree, to the contents of the famine code, which was prepared with great trouble by their Maharaja and superiors to give them light, to lessen their responsibilities, to define their duties, and to fortify their position. But, as so often, the wishes of the author were lost sight of, and the degree of order which he expected to evolve was frustrated by the ignorance and indifference of the executive, each individual of which preferred to set up a standard of his own, according to the measure of his own unaided common-sense, or, shall I say, no-sense.

I hope the notice of such laches taken during and after the tours, and the consequent measures adopted by Government, will minimise the effects of the ignorance displayed by the officials, who must perforce be the agents employed to carry out the responsible and arduous policy of Government.

Orders were issued to apply the task system to all the works in the Kadi division. The tasks prescribed by the earlier orders were revised with a view to prevent their being unduly light and, therefore, too attractive to the labourers.

The immediate result on the Gangadi tank was a sensible lowering in the numbers of relief-seekers. The daily average of attendance fell from 16,000 to half that number.

23. My attention having, as above stated, been drawn to the complaints made by the labourers on the relief-works, I set my mind to redress such of their grievances as seemed to me to be real. The complaints of the labourers relieved.

I had asked some of them, when I visited their work, to explain to me their wants and the manner in which they proposed to remedy them. Some were such dullards that they could hardly speak, though they were the foremost in complaining ; others did not know what they had to complain of; most were as little acquainted with the orders of Government as with their own duty and the principle of self-help. Again, and I mention it as the last but not the least of the difficulties I had to encounter, I had to face old men and women so anxious to sing their song of woe before him whom they looked on as their omnipotent Maharaja and Ma-Bap—the superhuman destroyer of all ills—that my ears were deafened, my attention distracted, by their different doleful ditties set to different tunes. I asked a few of both sexes to come to my residence and tell me freely their tale of misery, and, in accordance with my orders, the officer in charge of the work sent these delegates at the appointed hour to my place. There I listened to and took notes of their grievances, and, after feeding them and giving them each a rupee as bakshish, I told them that they might go, and that Government would do all that was possible to help them out of their misfortunes. Of course I received a plentiful shower of blessings and thanks, accompanied by voluble protestations that I could deal with them as I liked, that I was their master, that they were instinctively led to lay their grievances before me, and that I could dispose of their complaints as I pleased. All they hoped was that they should get sufficient to keep body and soul together, and this, they said, could be done by the grant of a daily dole of 2 lbs. of grain. One could not remain silent and unmoved in the presence of these simple, trusty folk, ignorant as yet of the tricks and ways of modern agitation, who thus displayed a novel, because so very old, reverence and love for their ruler.

Delay in payment of wages.

24. One of their complaints was that they did not receive regular and prompt payment for the work they did. The Public Works officers were questioned as to the cause of this grievance, which they admitted to be real. Ordinarily, according to the Public Works Code, payments have to be made in the presence of the cashier. There being a large number of works, and the number of cashiers being limited, the labourers had to await the advent of this officer before they could get their wages, and they were sometimes kept out of their earnings for a whole week. This rule was modified so as to suit the special requirements of the petitioners. Mistries and supervisors, after depositing the requisite security, were empowered to make the requisite disbursements.

How remedied.

25. To prevent irregularities or corrupt practices in the payment of wages, and to guarantee that the money should actually reach

the hands of the labourers, as well as to see that proper muster-rolls were kept and fair measurements made, special officers were appointed. Some of my own Mankaris were also deputed to do this work, but this was, partly, because I wished to emphasise the personal interest I took in the misfortunes of the people. To secure a greater number of well-qualified supervisors a class was specially opened, where instruction in taking measurements and keeping muster-rolls was imparted to military savars. Some of these saukars were deputed to the Kadi division to carry out the work to which I am referring.

Excessive tasks.

26. There was also a complaint that the weak and the infirm had sometimes to leave the works, as they could not possibly bring up their tale of work to the standard fixed. Orders were issued to the medical authorities to classify the labourers, and the task of each grade was differentiated, so as to be in proportion to the working capacity imposed by the code.

Low wages; Babashahi coin.

27. Another complaint was that the wages were paid in Babashahi copper coins. In the Kadi district Babashahi copper coins are not much in circulation in private trade transactions. The labourers, therefore, complained that they suffered loss, as the bazar people charged a heavy exchange rate on these copper coins. The Minister was instructed to see whether this payment in Babashahi could not with advantage be superseded by payment in British coppers. The Minister suggested that the ground of the labourers' complaint could be removed by providing some shops at which Babashahi coppers would be accepted without the imposition of an

undue exchange rate. Shops were accordingly provided where the rates of exchange were regulated and checked by the Vahivatdars from week to week. The Accountant-General was also instructed to send a sufficient supply of copper coins to the Kadi division for the purposes of payment, as too scanty a supply was an additional cause of delay. I hope these measures brought about the result expected by the labourers.

Holidays.

28. I directed that weekly holidays should be granted to children below fourteen, and fortnightly holidays on the new moon and full moon days to all labourers. This boon was much appreciated when it was first announced on the Gungadi work at Pattan. The attention of the local officers was also drawn to other minor grievances, in the hope that they would find means to redress them.

Sheds and resting-places.

29. The large sum of 4000 rupees was also placed at the disposal of each of the Subhas of Kadi, Baroda, and Amreli, for the erection of sheds and temporary mandwas (sheds) to shelter infirm and aged people as well as infants on the scene of the relief-works. I shall watch to see what use will be made of these grants. The real necessity for sheds was felt in January, when the weather was especially inclement and cold, and I shall be only too glad to learn that this grant has been utilised to protect the poor people from the rigour of the season.

Feeling for the misery these unfortunate creatures would have to endure during the season of dry cold winds, I ordered clothes to be distributed among the men, women, and children at

RELIEF-WORK AT PATAN

[Face page 22.

the works in Kadi. I hope the execution of my order has supplied the wants of those who really needed the gift.

30. Next to the complaints of the labourers on the relief-works, those of the people at large engaged my serious attention. The Minister and my secretary, besides being required to do so by standing orders, were particularly instructed to receive and to listen patiently to all sorts of applications from the people at all places visited during my tour. General nature of complaints.

To enable petitioners the more easily to find their way, a notice-board was set up in a public place to guide them to the office. In addition to this I used to send for the petitioners myself. The applications received during this tour numbered 632, and the points of their grievances may be broadly classified under the following three main heads. Demands were made :—

(*a*) For remission or suspension of assessment due to the Sarkar ;

(*b*) For tagavi advances for the sinking of wells, or for seed, or for maintenance ;

(*c*) For tagavi for grass, wherewith to feed the cattle. Other miscellaneous requests were made, begging for gifts, presents, even scholarships; and complaints were brought against local officers, etc.

31. Nearly 75 per cent of the applications were for the remission or suspension of the assessment. This important question was already under consideration. The State was straining every nerve to preserve life, and was freely parting with all its savings to provide work for the destitute. In other words, the call for assist- Assessment and its remission.

ance was immense, the resources of Government not limitless. My first anxious thought was to support the distressed rayats; my second thought, scarcely less anxious, was to avoid incurring debt. The evils of indebtedness are patent to all. Rumours were afloat that the British Government, with its usual alertness, was going to take advantage of this dire time to persuade or force the native Rajas to borrow money from or through them. The first object, however, prevailed, and the State has been sanctioning lakhs upon lakhs to support the distressed people. With so large an expenditure it would tax the ablest financier to arrange for the remission or suspension of the land-tax. Orders were, however, issued to cease from all coercive measures, and my officers were instructed to see that no undue pressure was employed, as well as to assure themselves that only those who had the means to do so and a direct interest in the land should be called on to pay. It is easy to understand that, though such were inconsistent with the terms of our Land Revenue Settlement, petitions for the remission or suspension of the land-tax for the current year and, sometimes, of arrears were profusely made throughout the Raj by a class which is conscious of its importance to the State, providing it as it does with almost the whole of its income, without which the machinery of administration cannot work. Such being its high status in its relation with the State, the agricultural class requested, demanded, almost insisted on indulgent treatment, and eventually some of its members urged on Government the necessity for wholly abandoning all attempts to recover the land assessment during the year, professing themselves willing to pay the following year. I balanced the exceptional nature of the season with the various benevolent steps taken by the State to mitigate the severity of our misfortune, and found that the agricultural class deserved to obtain some favourable attention from Government. The problem before me seemed to be as follows :—

On the one side : (1) the State undertakes to pay an enhanced rate of salary to its varied and large class of low-paid servants.

(2) It feeds and maintains the infirm, the aged, and the orphan.

(3) It finds work for the able-bodied members of a class which comes into close contact with, and even to a certain extent is indispensable to, the agriculturist, but which is certainly not the agricultural class.

(4) It finds money to advance loans to the class of Girasias, Ek-ankadi, and Farta-ankadi Jamindars, to copper-smiths and to the respectable poverty-stricken portion of the population.

On the other side the question that naturally arises is, whether Government does enough for that class of its subjects, which, not merely from a humanitarian point of view, but from an economical standpoint, deserves far more liberal treatment than is accorded it at present. Whether Government can do more, and in what manner it should do so, are points which I do not undertake to solve ; but I strongly feel that the agriculturists do not get the generous treatment accorded to the other classes, who do not contribute so much to Government as do the Kheduts—the mainstay of Government, and 80 per cent of our population. Let it be clearly understood that I am not, out of any petty jealousy, running down the propriety of according benevolent and humane treatment to the other classes. All that I assert is, that our one really useful class should be treated, if not more liberally, at least not worse than others who are maintained by the money the former give to the State, and who thrive and prosper in a country like India mainly through the exertions of the cultivators. It may easily be conceived that I was inclined to lend a sympathetic ear to the entreaties of the cultivators, and that I have tried to meet their wishes as far as it has lain in my power, though the indulgence granted had not reached the point I should have liked it to attain had I been in a better position, or in possession of other sources of income than those supplied by the land. In a Native State, where the transit dues, port dues, and a salt revenue are non-existent, while traffic and trade are, to say the least, limited, where expenses are all on the increase, now that the ideas of Government are undergoing a change, and are tending towards greater expense, a Raja has to think more than once before he surrenders his only important source of revenue. He is deterred, again, by the danger of debt and the servitude to which the State would consequently be reduced. I have endeavoured, notwithstanding all these fears and misgivings, to deal with the peasants as liberally as possible within circumscribed limits. I have frequently in a single day interviewed more than one deputation of fifty or more petitioners, and discussed with them the difficulty in which we were placed. I have argued and explained to them the position of Government, and always found them willing to pay the closest attention to my words, and able to criticise them as wise and practical, if humble, men of the world. And I have tried to meet their wishes as much as I could. Throughout my different tours, undertaken for different purposes and at different times, I have come into contact with the cultivator class, and I have found that its collective common-sense, when unexcited and dispassionate, is generally correct, and such as deserves serious consideration before it is dropped or pooh-poohed. It is easier to deal with them than with their self-styled representatives as we find them in the Council Hall of Governors and in the courts of justice—men who have picked up the declamation, the harangue, the notions, perhaps the sentiments of the West. These gentlemen are, in their turn, fast becoming the guides of the naturally credulous peasants, who are too far removed from their legitimate rulers to understand the latter or to be understood by them.

Advantages of sinking wells.

32. The next general complaint was that they had not received tagavi advances for wells, seed, etc. Kadi is a district in which there are exceptional facilities for sinking wells. The advantages of getting such wells sunk by tagavi advances are many :—

(1) They secure the country to some extent against the ravages of a real famine, and most certainly are a guarantee against the frequent recurrence of times of scarcity.

(2) The very construction of wells for irrigation gives employment to a goodly number

of men. It has been found by experience that each new well affords work to an average of seven men, while irrigation by means of an old well affords it to about three men. So many therefore are saved the necessity of seeking relief on State works.

(3) The cultivator who borrows tagavi is able to maintain himself and his family on this well-sinking work independently of State relief, and thus learns the value of self-reliance. The crops he is able to turn out provide food for himself, his family, and his cattle. Wells, I repeat, give a healthy opening for independent employment, and are themselves a security against the horrors of famine.

Tagavi for seeds.

33. Orders were also given to grant tagavi for the purchase of seeds and agricultural implements. 50,000 rupees were sanctioned for this purpose as the season for the winter crops was well upon us. These advances of tagavi, it is hoped, have enabled the cultivators to purchase seed and raise some winter crops by irrigation.

Tagavi to the Mewasi villages.

34. A separate sum of 15,000 rupees was also sanctioned for giving tagavi to the Mewasi villages, though they could not claim any such help under the ordinary revenue rules. The Mewasis agreed that in default of repayment their lands might be sold like ordinary Sarkari lands, and, on this security, Mewasi holders were declared eligible for help.

35. The next main difficulty of the cultivator lay in his utter inability to keep his cattle alive. Government had adopted several measures with a view to preserve live stock, the mainstay of our agricultural population. The people

clamoured most for the preservation of the cattle, not only because they were their chief helpmates in all agricultural pursuits, but also because these beasts were cherished from sentiments of religion, both by the Hindus and the Jains, the latter forming an influential section of the population of North Gujarat.

Tagavi for the raising of grass and fodder; facilities for grazing.

(*a*) Government had thrown open certain waste lands for the cultivation of fodder.

(*b*) It had set certain tracts of forests free for grazing purposes. Large numbers of cattle were allowed to be transported to the Songadh forests that they might support themselves there.

(*c*) It had allowed head-loads of forest produce to be removed free of charge, both for cattle and men.

(*d*) It had exempted certain articles of food for cattle from the usual customs duties.

(*e*) It had held out a promise of two rupees per bigha as a reward for fodder cultivation of any kind.

36. Notwithstanding these endeavours, the mortality among the cattle was high, and an abnormal number died at the very first shock. To preserve those that remained, it was directed that tagavi in grass should be given to any cultivator who had cattle and who applied for such help.

Grass from Songadh.

Knowing the advantage of measures to preserve cattle, I had, at the very commencement, evinced great interest in the question, and taken much trouble to supply the cultivators with as large a supply of fodder as possible. But I had left the execution of the orders and of details to the Minister and the Famine Commissioner.

The Khetiwadi Kamdar and other officers were asked to arrange for the cutting and transport of grass from the Songadh forests. When I went to Kadi, I found that only small quantities of grass had been transported to that district; and the people, who, it was said, had relied upon the Khetiwadi Kamdar's assurances, were much disappointed and dismayed at the failure of the promised supply—a supply which only began to come in after many of the cattle had already died. At the same time whole waggon-loads of grass, which on inquiry were found to be mostly from our Tapti Valley, were being exported to distant places. The mismanagement and trouble connected with our attempt to supply the people with grass deserve to be borne in mind, so that we may not repeat the follies which were perpetrated this year by the forest, agricultural, and military departments.

I may here incidentally mention that the vagaries and tricks that were used to get out of the conditions of the contract made by the military contractors were mentioned to me, when the contract was given by some officials to the people of Ahmadabad; but I had attributed the remarks to prejudice and trade rivalry.

I directed that a stop should be put to irregularities in the sale of grass imported from Songadh by transferring the whole business of the sale of grass to the Vahivatdars, who were to be assisted by teachers, Nodhani Kamdars, and other Government servants. They were enjoined to see that the grass was fairly distributed without any favouritism and at a reasonable price, so that the purchase of grass might be within the means of all cultivators.

37. The last subject to which I turned my attention was a series of representations made me by the local officials.

Complaints of local officers; how remedied.

(1) Their one important complaint was that prompt reply was not made to their requisitions by the Huzur officers, and that their correspondence was not carefully gone into.

(2) That the sanctions were delayed, and that they themselves were often left to continue certain works on their own responsibility.

(3) That the Huzur officers, without much acquaintance with local needs, frequently changed their plan of campaign without any apparent reason.

To remedy these grievances, I used often to talk personally with the local officers, and explain to them the salient features in the policy of the Huzur, so as to clear up any misunderstanding. And further, to get rid of some of the evils mentioned, and especially that of delay arising from the necessity for demanding sanction from several officials, I took certain steps to be noted later. I argued that the higher officers could not be expected to do more than a good and experienced officer well versed in the wants of his particular district would, if only he had the energy to travel, for he had the best opportunity of noting the real needs of the people.

From the start, I had constituted a famine bureau at the Huzur, with an officer at its head armed with sufficient power to correct any abuses and to supervise, by constant travelling, the execution of the orders of Government. I had often to press this officer to travel in the district, or, if he could not himself do so, at least to send out his second-in-command. As a matter of fact, I believe the latter hardly ever forsook the charms of headquarters except to push the grass business, with the execution of which he ought to have been the last person to be entrusted. These remarks, which are made in a friendly spirit, will, I hope, have the effect of inducing certain gentlemen to take to seeing things for themselves, rather than pass their time in filling up vast forms or in piling up bundles of returns.

The other complaints of local officers were :—

(1) The want of adequate and competent machinery ;

(2) The paucity of schemes, and of establishments to mature further schemes to meet the demands made upon them by the higher officers. The latter, it was urged by the local subordinates, kept asking for "new works" without appreciating the difficulty of creating plans and suggestions.

Another thing I noticed with regard to local officials was that they often betrayed great ignorance of the rules of the code and of Huzur orders, though they excused themselves, and sometimes justifiably, by pleading that they had not received any clear information or any copy of the orders passed by the Huzur. Sometimes, too, they complained of a want of zealous support from their superiors, who were unduly nervous of the Huzur. I was very glad to meet these local officials personally, for from them I learned their view of the question, and sometimes picked up valuable hints which enabled me to make some reforms and to judge comprehensively of the whole subject. Knowing as I do the danger of generalising and of passing remarks on our services as a whole—services which are very diverse—I may yet say that there can be found among the local officers men who, though they may be subject to the common infirmity of rating themselves higher than they really are, have in them the making of really efficient and capable servants. But they must be led in the right direction by strict and efficient supervision, and they, in their turn, must keep themselves aloof from the fascination of political speculation, and must learn to look up to and be controlled by the one authority from whom alone they should expect applause or censure.

Discretionary grants of 3000 rupees in each case, and up to 20,000 rupees in the aggregate, were given to the Subha and to the Executive Engineer conjointly, in order that immediate action might be taken by the local officers without preliminary sanction from higher authorities —a sanction too frequently retarded by cumbrous red-tapeism.

Programmes of relief-works were discussed in the presence of the local officers, to whose grievances a ready hearing was promised.

Subhas freed from their ordinary Revenue work.

38. The Subhas were freed from their ordinary Revenue duties and directed to work as assistants to the Famine Commissioner in their own districts. They were from time to time vested with large discretionary powers to incur expenditure in the conduct of the various famine operations.

D

AMRELI DIVISION

LABOURERS' HUTS AT VISNAGAR

[Face page 37.

II.—AMRELI DIVISION

1. After having satisfied myself as to the state of affairs and the condition of relief-works in the Kadi division, I proceeded in the early part of this year to Amreli, where the failure of rain had been as complete and the prevailing distress as great as in the north. I visited Damnagar, Amreli, Dhari, Khamba, and Kodinar. *Amreli tour. 15/1/1900 to 2/2/1900.*

2. Damnagar appeared to be the least affected district on the Kathiawad side. The condition of the people on the relief-works was not so poor as elsewhere. The cattle also looked comparatively healthy. The cool and bracing climate of Damnagar must have had the effect of keeping up the physique of the people. The private charity of some Mahajans was also greatly instrumental in maintaining the cheerfulness of this little town. Mr. Keshavalal and his brother have deserved well of their country for utilising their wealth in the support of their less fortunate brethren. Damnagar, I should add, was also more lucky than other parts of Amreli in having had a little more rain. *Damnagar.*

3. The main difficulty we had to contend with in the Amreli division was the paucity of big useful works which might momentarily employ a large number of labourers and at the *Complaints about works.*

same time be of permanent advantage to the country. The object of a famine programme should be not only to provide immediate work for those who need relief, but also to make it of a kind to develop the country—in other words, be remunerative and useful in preventing future famines, or at least in mitigating their horror. Roads and tanks have their own local uses and purposes; but beyond such limited usefulness, they hardly subserve any object of permanent benefit. Roads in a rocky country like Kathiawad are not much needed by the village people, and yet roads formed the sole prominent feature of the relief-works in Amreli.

Programme of relief-works.

4. Just as the prevailing characteristic of the relief-works in Kadi was the number of small tanks that were being excavated, so roads made up the item which figured conspicuously on the Amreli programme. My chief criticism, therefore, in this division regarded the nature of the works to be constructed. I discussed the scheme prepared by the Minister and the Famine Commissioner with the Sar Subha and the local officers. Then, with the concurrent advice of the Subha and the Executive Engineer, a programme was definitely settled, and some new works were suggested for this division. The opinions and suggestions of intelligent and influential men of the district were also invited, to enable Government to arrive at a useful and practical plan of campaign. Amongst these local advisers the Vakeels, as usual, figured conspicuously; next to them came the Banias. In spite, however, of all these endeavours, the

programme, even as finally settled, remained far from satisfactory.

Difficulties found in framing it.

5. If we seek to discover the reasons of its imperfections they will not be far to seek. The main difficulties that beset us in our efforts to develop the list of works can be classified under two comprehensive heads.

(*A*) Political.

(*B*) Professional.

The Amreli Chital Railway.

6. (*A*) The railway from Chital (Khijaria) to Amreli, and thence on to Chalala and Dhari, would have been a useful item in the relief programme for Amreli. The attitude of the British Government, however, was against the retention by Baroda of jurisdiction on this line, even though it is an isolated and local line. We could not expect the supreme Government to be over-anxious to meet our wishes, unless we urged our legitimate claims upon their notice in the form of a respectful protest. The railway would have proved a most opportune relief for a district wanting in other facilities for works of a useful nature, but, as I have said, we have to take into consideration the attitude assumed by the British Government. Subsequently I learnt that the Government of India had refused their permission to the construction of this line, even though it was practically an isolated one. Most unwillingly, therefore, I had to abandon a work which promised to be a most useful one, because I could not surrender a State right.

Amreli Railway.

(1) I have to thank the Resident for the promptness with which the decision of the Government of India was communicated. It is, however, a pity that the British Government is

so fond of centralisation, and so strictly compels Native States to ask for its sanction in matters where they ought to be entirely free to make their own arrangements, even, if necessary, in concert with other neighbouring Native States. If Native States are to be preserved in all their vitality, it is necessary to give them greater freedom, and promote in them habits of self-reliance, and to stop this policy of chaperoning done out of mistaken kindness. Some blunders are preferable to imbecility and want of timely decision.

The tendency of the British authorities in their treatment of Native Administrations, in periods of famine, seems at times too assertive of supremacy. This proclivity tends to create a gulf between the Native governors and the governed, and all manly interest in the pursuit of good and consistent rule is discouraged.

(2) I have long been anxious in the interests of progress and civilisation to give this rocky and sparsely-inhabited country good means of communication, and on my return from Amreli it occurred to me that for the present, at least, a tramway, which could at any time be converted into a railway, would meet the requirements of the country almost as efficiently as a railway. I have accordingly sanctioned the widening of the existing road, and I hope that before long a well-managed tramway will be in existence. The laying down of rails is a matter of financial consideration, and has little to do with famine measures. That portion of the work which is likely to be useful as a famine work is already in progress.

7. Then there is the scheme for the improve-

ment of the Velan Port. The harbour at Velan is naturally so well fitted to afford shelter and protection to ships, that, with some initial outlay, it might readily be turned into a very useful haven of refuge. The neighbouring bunders have no such natural advantages, and Velan might possibly be able to draw away traffic from several Kathiawad ports. The Chief Engineer has submitted two schemes for the improvement of Velan, but before we go in for so large an outlay as is required for the thorough execution of the scheme, it would be prudent to feel our way, and see that our position as regards Kathiawad ports is secure.

Velan Bunder improvement. The Gir road.

A road proposed to be constructed between Dhari and Kodinar through the Gir is a huge undertaking, and is not likely to be taken up owing to its prohibitive cost, even if no political difficulties interposed themselves.

8. (*B*) But apart from these difficulties not quite within our control, there were others which prevented our including large useful works in the Amreli programme. There were two irrigation projects deemed feasible, viz. one on the Shetrunja River, and another on the Shingands near Ghatwad in Kodinar. The Public Works Department had no schemes ready for these two works, and it was not likely that, with their existing staff, they would be able to mature a project in time to enable us to carry it through during the season of distress.

Professional difficulties. Irrigation schemes.

I also suggested the idea of constructing a reservoir near Mota Bhandaria on the road to Dhari, and asked that the scheme should be worked out along with such other irrigational projects as might suggest themselves. Later on, I learnt that some of the last-named works could not profitably be undertaken, thus reducing the scope of the programme. This want of possible big schemes must have resulted in the adoption of many a makeshift, and have caused many an anxious moment to those who took a legitimate and intelligent interest in the successful execution of the famine policy. In case another famine occurs, the State will find it extremely difficult to discover useful relief-projects, as works like the construction of roads and railways, drainage schemes, and certain projects of irrigation, are being rapidly pushed on, and will be completed in a few years. The component parts of the division are scattered, and its sole dependence is upon agriculture. This will render any future famine administration most expensive and difficult. Above all, any policy, however good it may be, will fail if the British authorities are not in sympathy with it.

Strengthening the Public Works service.

9. As I have already remarked in my notes on the Kadi tour, I had noticed there the complaint that there was a want of sufficient and efficient hands, and in Amreli the evil was intensified. Mr. Parbhudas, the permanent ex-Engineer, told me that he had in vain written to his superiors on the necessity for more hands. It struck me here how lacking some of the Public Works officers were in ability to initiate measures and suggestions, and how lethargic they were. To strengthen the Department, two more engineers were added to the two already on the staff. Messrs. Pavri and Trivedi were deputed to assist Messrs. Lallubhai and Parbhudas.

The higher officers of the Public Works Department also complained of a want of hands for surveying and taking levels, and pleaded their inability to push on projects without such extra help. Orders were given to start a class where instruction should be imparted to about a hundred men in this elementary branch of engineering. But one hundred men! It would be no easy matter to get so large a number of fairly intelligent men together, and the training of them would be both expensive and slow. Later on, I was naturally asked to reduce the number to a more manageable and economical figure, and this I was glad to do. I had, before the famine had made much progress, thought of drawing upon some of the State services for men who could safely be lent to the Public Works. I had on several occasions mentioned the matter to the Senapati, and ultimately I instructed him to train a number of his men to assist in the famine relief-works. While in Baroda I evinced my interest in this little measure by making occasional inquiries regarding the progress of the class which was formed, and by paying a visit to their school, though I was hard pressed for time owing to my multifarious engagements. I was glad to find that my idea of training a few outside men was appreciated by the Public Works Department officers in Kathiawad.

Additional hands.

The men turned out by this school were directed to assist in the work of surveying and taking levels. Some savars from the Military Department, coached up in the work of supervision, were also lent to the Public Works Department. The Educational Inspector was also ordered to detail teachers from schools where the attendance of pupils had dwindled owing to the famine, to learn supervision work in order to assist the Public Works Department, and in this way to supply the want of hands to a certain extent. Unfortunately the Educational Inspector was unable to do much.

Tagavi for well-sinking.

10. In the absence of large and useful irrigation and railway projects—the most efficient channels for the development of the resources of the country and for the mitigation of future famines—the Government had to fall back upon the plan of getting numerous wells sunk by tagavi advances. A large amount had already been set apart for this purpose, and a special officer from the Khangi Department, Mr. Appa Saheb Mohite, employed on the distribution of the money. This officer proved himself to be both intelligent and energetic. He was, moreover, able to come into close contact with the people, of whom he seemed to have an intimate knowledge, and with whom he had warm sympathies. I went quietly in company with this officer to see how a well was constructed—a process which appeared to involve a lot of physical labour and loss of instruments. Eventually people were invited to make fresh demands for tagavi to sink wells if they had not already received such help. It was observed at Damnagar and Dhari that many cultivators were anxious to avail themselves of the facilities thus offered them, and orders were given sanctioning a further allotment of 5000 rupees for Damnagar Mahal and of 14,000 rupees for the Dhari Taluka.

11. The sinking of a well would, it was

calculated, employ at least six or seven labourers; and consequently, if a large number of wells were simultaneously sunk, the operation would appreciably relieve the plethora of workmen at the ordinary centres of relief. The works in the Amreli division were liberally patronised by the relief-seekers, and the daily average of attendance had run up to 32,000 when I was at Amreli. This was a large number for the population of the division: the percentage of relief-seekers to the entire population of Amreli, including Okhamandal, had, in fact, actually reached 25 per cent. This naturally inspired some doubts as to the correctness of the principle on which relief was afforded to the people.

Wells sunk by relief-labour.

(1) Indeed, the distance test was not properly applied.

(2) Residence at night on the scene of work was not insisted upon.

(3) Large numbers of comparatively well-to-do men were seen to flock to our works, accompanied by relatives from foreign territories.

To regulate the movement, it was deemed necessary to divert the crowds from the relief-works and to get them employed on well-sinking. 22,000 rupees were sanctioned for the construction of fresh wells in Kodinar, and the special officer in charge of the taluka was instructed to see that the recipients of tagavi employed some men from the relief-works, more especially his own relations or caste-men.

Of course the operation of well-sinking would require some labourers who were adepts in that line, and were accustomed to work in water;

but after making liberal provision for expert work, it was thought that the well-sinking operation would take a large number of hands off the relief-works.

Wells sunk at a Government expense of 2,50,000 rupees.

12. It was also observed that some cultivators had not sufficient credit to entitle them to tagavi advances, or were not anxious to run into debt by sinking wells with relief-labour. Many were eager, however, to reap all the benefits of the improved cultivation that would ensue from the construction of wells at Government expense. To meet their wishes, the amount spent by Government was to be a charge upon the land having a priority over every other charge, being treated, that is to say, as Government assessment. Many cultivators expressed their readiness to pay the increased assessment that would be charged on their holdings, though they were not prepared to borrow a tagavi advance. They were prepared to employ labourers from the relief-works on the construction of their well.

To carry out its object of lessening the pressure on the relief-works, the Huzur sanctioned the large expenditure of two lakhs and a half on the construction of wells at the expense of the State and under State supervision. Three special officers were employed, one in each of the remaining talukas of the Amreli division, to supervise this important undertaking. It was calculated that the improvement effected in the condition of the agricultural holdings would indirectly make the investment a profitable one, as the improved cultivation of the soil would eventually increase the State assessment, while it would enrich the cultivator, ensure him against future scarcity, and assist him even in famine years.

Number and nature of relief-works in progress.

13. At the time of my tour through the division there was a large number of relief-works going on. I am almost correct in saying that each Taluka and Peta-mahal was supplied with two or three, all simultaneously at work. There were about thirty-five works in Amreli and Okhamandal in the week ending 15th January. They consisted mainly of road-making and metal-breaking in Amreli, Dhari, Okha, and Kodinar, while some tanks were being excavated in Damnagar and Okhamandal. There were no works of a remunerative character or of permanent utility; and the percentage of relief-seekers to the entire population had reached the high figure mentioned at paragraph 11. The works were often opened too near the villages and homesteads of the labourers, who were undeterred by social sentiment of any kind from resorting to the so-called relief centres and from availing themselves of State charity.

Distance test.

14. Considering the state of the season and the stage of distress, the percentage of attendance appeared to me abnormal, and, as a judicious check on the movement, I ordered the distance test to be applied. This was accordingly done in Damnagar, where the condition of the people appeared tolerable, so that the experiment could safely be made there. When a distance test is enforced, only those who are really pinched by distress elect to leave their homes and to reside on the works themselves. I was told that, as a result of the application of the test, the numbers fell off.

I must add that I began with Damnagar, because one has to be careful in passing orders on such matters, as they are apt to be misunderstood. They are misrepresented by interested parties, whose tales find ready credence with ignorant people. The Subha, who is a travelled and well-educated man, and an officer who has seen much service, could be safely trusted to carry out my purpose, and to watch its evolution in a way to prevent any mischief arising.

Complaints on the works.

15. After I had settled the programme of relief-works for the Amreli division, and remedied to some extent the complaints of the Executive officers about the works, I directed my attention towards the complaints made by the people on these very works.

Agricultural class described.

And here let me say a word regarding their appearance :—

The males of the agricultural class, taken *en masse*, seemed to be naturally stalwart and well made. They were almost invariably clad in loose blouses of a dirty white, with short, rough, home-spun khadi coats, while on the head they wore a scarf, folded in the peculiar Kathiawadi fashion. Not a few of them—and this refers to the women as well as the men—had well-proportioned features and possessed a fair and pleasing complexion.

The labourers on the relief-works complained of the heavy tasks exacted of them. On looking into the matter, I found that the average labourer earned a subsistence wage only, and hardly one of their number was able to accomplish the first-class task. The metal-breaking task imposed was of exceptional severity, and very few could earn even the minimum wage allotted. Similar complaints had been communicated by the Okhamandal authorities. So I asked the Minister to revise and lighten the standard of work, in consultation with the Chief Engineer.

16. In consequence of the heavy tasks imposed, the wages earned were so low as to form the constant theme of the labourers' petitions. It was hoped that when the tasks were lightened this ground of complaint would disappear. Low wages.

I must not be understood to imply that the cry regarding heavy tasks and low wages was peculiar to this division. It was universal within and without the limits of the Baroda Raj. The labourers, though they were, and still continue to be, meek enough, are, owing to the conduct of Government and from contact with people like Vakeels, schoolmasters, and Government servants, learning to believe that it is the duty of Government to save life at any cost. And who are the people into whose minds such a notion is being sedulously introduced? They are people of an indolent nature, who live under the scorching sun and in the relaxing damp of the plains of Gujarat, men who, even in prosperous years, have to be goaded on to work, and who do their best to avoid exerting themselves whenever they possibly can. Not a few of the famine-stricken people much prefer begging to earning their livelihood in an honest and honourable way.

True as I believe the remark I have just made to be, I felt that there was something faulty in the standard of work fixed by the Engineers.

The question was whether various kinds of work were sufficiently differentiated.

One word more before I quit the subject. It is right to note that though the labourers were loud and unanimous in their complaint, the Public Works officers, let it be said to their credit, strongly protested that even under the existing rules the work turned out was very unsatisfactory. The cost to Government was unnecessarily heavy ; and the officers found fault with the minimum wage system. I paid due attention to both sides of the question, and eventually issued orders that the piece-work system should be introduced—a system in which I have not yet lost faith. It is very demoralising and almost as foolish to treat well-to-do labourers with leniency, as it is cruel and unpleasant to be unduly hard upon those who have become physically feeble. Besides, the system before in vogue was unnecessarily complicated and left much to the discretion of officers and low-paid subordinates—a class of people who, very naturally, are not distinguished as original thinkers, as organisers, or even as independent actors, who often lack interest in their work, often lack the power to express what may be their thoughts regarding their difficulties. An administrator has at times to surbordinate his high ideals to the capacity of the tools he uses. To what an extent this is the case in our community, and in Native States generally, can only be fully realised by those who have constantly to deal with them.

The condition of people in Khambha.

17. On the road from Ingorala to Khambha the condition of the labourers seemed very

poor ; but the generally insalubrious climate of Khambha was mainly responsible for their poor appearance.

It makes a great difference if you see a thing yourself, or if you are compelled to receive on trust the impressions of others, who, often unwittingly, paint their picture in more vivid colours than the case requires. Again, different minds receive different impressions or different degrees of the same impression about any one particular occurrence. These discrepancies are common to us all ; and it is useless to attempt to set them quite right. In order to ascertain the material condition of the people and to gauge the degree of distress prevailing amongst them, I had inquired of the Kodinar Munsiff as to how many holdings had changed hands since the right of occupancy had been given to them, and I was gratified to learn that very few lands had been alienated. This is rather an instructive and interesting fact. I had also heard of the physical condition of the Amreli people, and I carefully watched their state whenever I happened to be amongst them. Throughout this tour I seldom saw individuals amongst the cultivators so badly off or so emaciated as some of the people of the Baroda division, or as the outsiders who had flocked in to the capital. The people who struck me during this tour as being physically the worst off were, first, the Kodinar, and secondly, the Khambha cultivators. The former looked dispirited and lazy ; the latter were not so badly off ; and even if they were to a certain extent below par, the cause lay partly in the insalubrious climate of the Peta-mahal. I rode rapidly over some forty miles of road to see the condition of the people of Khambha. On my way to and back, between this place and Dhari, I halted at several spots, and listened patiently to the groans and moans of the labourers, keenly watching their condition. I also witnessed the method of distributing work amongst the different labourers. Finding that it was a cold and windy day, I ordered the distribution of some clothes to the men, women, and children on the works. It was here that I was again struck by the fine, well-chiselled features, and the intelligent looks of some of the people at work, that betokened well-developed brains. Their fair complexion also proved that the people must at one time at least have belonged to a different race from the Hindus of Gujarat. The intrinsically valueless ornaments some of the women wore in their ears closely resembled those displayed by the Mohammedan women. I should guess from the general style of the adornments and the physical development of some among the crowd that they must originally have come to Kathiawar from the direction of Sindh.

Kitchen at Khambha.

18. I directed a kitchen to be opened on the Khambha-Ingorala road, where the infant children of labourers on the relief-work might be fed and maintained at the expense of the State. The payment of half an anna per diem to children below the age of seven seemed frequently to fail in keeping them properly nourished. A kitchen, it was hoped, would prove a more effective safeguard for the health and condition of these striplings. On the very sensible recommendation of the Subha, the amount

THE SIDDHPUR ANNAGRUHA

[*Face page* 53.

given to these little ones was subsequently increased.

When starting the kitchen, I requested the Subha to report to me within a fortnight on the results of the experiment. The report, a favourable one, was sent in, but unluckily not till long after the fortnight had elapsed. I wanted the kitchen to be started as an experiment, and if successful, as a prelude to the several other kitchens I should have to open as the hot season approached and the famine increased in severity. It was eventually ascertained that the system of cash payments to the infants was abused by the labourers, who did not employ the doles to the end proposed, or for the benefit of those for whom they were designed, but misappropriated them in several ways. The kitchen system, to be successful, must be economical, and under strong and strict supervision, a desideratum which is often lacking, for subordinates are apt to be weak-kneed and superiors to be careless.

Distribution of clothing to the labourers on works.

19. The week I stayed at Amreli and Dhari was marked by intense cold and biting chilly north winds. The labourers who were homeless and insufficiently clothed were obviously suffering from the inclemency of the weather. Clothes were ordered to be distributed to the labourers at Dhari and Kodinar, and a sum of 1500 rupees was sanctioned for this purpose.

Famine ward at the Amreli Hospital.

20. While I was at Amreli, it was represented to me that it was most necessary to open a famine hospital, as an asylum for the weak and the famished, as well as for those who were

incapacitated from work by temporary indisposition. Some accommodation had to be provided for this purpose, and I ordered a ward of the Amreli Hospital, which had been unoccupied, to be set apart and placed exclusively at the disposal of the famine authorities.

Sheds for the labourers.

21. 4000 rupees had already been sanctioned for the purpose of constructing temporary sheds for the protection of the labourers from exposure at night. Hardly anywhere during my tour did I see good arrangements made for the housing of these unfortunate creatures. Frequently, however, and in this respect luckily, their work lay not far from their villages and homesteads, so that they could repair to them as often as possible, the distance test being practically non-existent. I had directed my chief medical officer, who happened to be in attendance on me, to visit these people and watch their condition carefully, to do all that was needful for them, as far as it lay in his power, and to report to me about anything beyond it. I had particularly impressed on Dr. Shamshuddin the necessity for watching the results of exposure on the physical system of these famine-stricken people. In order that we might draw the necessary conclusions by comparing the statistics of their health with those of ordinary years, I had told him to report to me the result of his observations, as I wished to see if my impressions about the absence of evil effects from want of sheds were right or wrong. I had asked him to mention his conclusions freely and not be influenced by my views. Indeed, I often fear to express a surmise even, as the merest hint is, at times,

made a cover for multitudes of sins by designing and unfit persons. I am not implying that the worthy Dr. Shamshuddin should be ranked among such people ; but I do assert that I have frequently to hold my tongue, so long as I think it immature to speak. I think the Subha was rather dilatory in providing these people with sheds, as he had not done so until the cold weather was almost disappearing. It is wonderful what time it takes to move bodies of officers to do anything of magnitude. The Subha represented that these sheds might be constructed from gunny bags and coarse cloth instead of from bamboo matting, as the supply of the coarse cloth for the purpose would itself afford some employment to the Amreli weavers.

A tagavi amount of 5000 rupees was also sanctioned for the Amreli weavers, to help them in their trade, as had previously been done in the case of the copper-smiths at Visnagar and the carpenters and blacksmiths of Shiyanagar, for whom 4000 rupees had been sanctioned.

The literature, consisting of the impressions, reflections, ideas, and schemes found in the Famine Commissioners' reports, and at times in newspapers, of what was being done in British territories had a great educational effect on the minds of our English-speaking officials ; and they often wanted to imitate and carry out exactly what they found was being done in British territory. This they often did to guard themselves against any unfavourable criticism. But sometimes their longing to follow suit was wanting in the discrimination which would have counselled some omissions. I may cite a case in point. The leaders of the weavers, as well as their saukars, and the weavers themselves, seemed to be quite willing to do anything for payment by the State. In fact, they preferred to do manual labour on relief-works rather than accept tagavi advances, and I can well understand the wise determination of these people. But the Subha seemed to wish to treat them in a way somewhat similar to that vouchsafed to the weavers of Sholapur. I am far from finding fault with the Subha or his objects. I only mention the fact and my views on it.

Complaints away from works.

22. The last kind of complaints that I sought to redress had nothing to do with the relief-works, but touched the wants of certain classes of people kept away from the relief-works either by social sentiment or by peculiar industrial pursuits. Such complaints were generally embodied in the applications which I received personally, or instructed my secretary to collect from the people. I had always arranged to see large batches of Patels and Girasias during this tour, and in my interesting interviews with them I tried to inform myself as to their thoughts and ideas about the measures to be adopted for mitigating the general distress. I invited suggestions from them as to any new projects for works which they deemed feasible in their own districts.

It would be as well to give a tangible share in the famine administration to such of my subjects as are respectable and sensible enough to take interest in it. The past policy of Native States will prove to us that this line of action is quite consistent with our traditions. The rulers-

and the ruled had then a closer bond of union, which it behoves us to preserve and cherish as much as we can.

The main complaints put forward can be classified under the three following heads :—

(*A*) Remission or suspension of the Government dues.

(*B*) Applications for further advances of tagavi for wells, or seed, or for maintenance.

(*C*) Applications for help towards the preservation of the cattle.

There were, besides these, other miscellaneous local topics. In all, the number of applications presented to me was 396.

Complaints: how remedied.

23. Of these complaints some were already remedied by the orders I had issued soon after my tour through the Kadi division. The general question of remission and suspension of revenue demands had been discussed with the Minister and the Sar Subha. All coercive measures for the realisation of the land revenue had been ordered to be dropped. The policy settled upon was to the effect that money was to be realised from those only who were in a position to give, while, as far as possible, no undue pressure was to be placed on those who were really helpless. Many of the complaints and requests for remission and suspension of revenue dues which I received were in anticipation of the coming revenue instalments. It can easily be understood that the policy of Government has to be carried out in detail by officers of various grades, salaries, and powers, who possess in various degrees the authority necessary to carry out Government orders more or less effectively,

while they have also greater or less opportunities of troubling the people. When dealing with the widespread interests of its subjects, all that Government can do is to minimise the scope and chances of hardship. Now the main point of the requests made by almost all the cultivators throughout the districts in which I travelled was that the Government should declare the proportion of its usual revenue it had determined to realise during this famine period. An experiment might have been made to comply with this request, but for certain reasons I did not think it was essential to interfere with the orders already issued. Rayats everywhere, and particularly in Native States, cry out before they are hurt. An exaggerated idea of zulum is thereby conveyed to the minds of people ignorant of the true state of things. But it is a fact well known to all experienced persons, though probably it may not be expressed in so many words, that a pookar or cry of complaint has an undue effect upon Native State officers and administrators. It is not to be understood from this that one should not keep his eyes and ears open and should not at times analyse complaints and do the needful to redress them. In British territory the people know that they have to deal with strong, vigorous, and powerful officers, supported by a strong and alien hierarchy of officials, who are backed up in their action by a strong, puissant Government, against whom no appeal or complaint would avail. The prestige of that Government is much higher than that of our tottering Native States. Notwithstanding all our generous desire to help the poor cultivators, we could ill afford to forgo the only important source of the State receipts, especially in a year like the present, when the drain on its coffers had been enormously heavy.

24. Large amounts for tagavi advances were sanctioned for the promotion of the construction of wells, and 20,000 rupees were also sanctioned for tagavi advances destined for the purchase of seed and other accessories of cultivation. Tagavi for seed.

25. Demands for tagavi for maintenance mostly emanated from the "beggared respectable" classes, who would die the horrible death of starvation rather than resort to relief-works. The Girasias of Amreli and Dhari represented this class, and they were quite reluctant to accept the proffered State help in the form of wages for work. Tagavi for maintenance for the Girasias.

26. These respectable poor had no credit to fall back upon, and no money-lender was likely to advance any sum to them on their own personal security. Their lands or Giras had long been steeped in debt, and they felt the sore pinch of the season very acutely. Numbers of them applied for State loans. The Sar Subha was directed to frame rules by which the State could ask the saukar to lend further amounts to such Girasias, after undertaking to assist the lenders to recover such amounts in the same manner as it would recover its own dues, and after assigning priority to claims for amounts lent under these new rules over all other private claims of other creditors. If the money-lenders refused to grant such loans, the State would advance amounts up to 300 rupees; claiming priority of recovery for such amounts, which would be Loans from money-lenders to Girasias.

regarded as so many charges on the land of the Girasias.

The action of the Kathiawad Political Agent in this respect served to initiate this policy and to strengthen our hands in its execution.

We are fast losing the power to govern, and are beginning to distrust ourselves so much that we fear to take a small step like this, for reasons right or wrong, unless we can convince ourselves that an exactly similar step has been taken by a high European officer or has been justified by European writers of great repute.

It is to be hoped that the needy Girasias will avail themselves of the help afforded by these rules, and that they will be of material assistance to them in the sore struggle they are waging.

Tagavi for grass.

27. The third main point mentioned in the petitions regarded the preservation of cattle. In other districts tagavi for this purpose had been ordered to be paid in kind, as there was great difficulty in the cultivator's procuring grass for himself, and also because there was the danger of his misappropriating the money and converting it to other uses. In Amreli, however, many cultivators had grown crops of sugar-cane, etc., which would afford fodder for their cattle, and the applicants were desirous of getting cash tagavi so as to enable them to purchase other articles of consumption for their cattle. Very possibly the petitioners had other objects in view.

There were no great facilities for importing grass into this district, and it was not found convenient to transport grass from the Tapti valley to so great a distance. Arrangements could have been made to transport grass by ships to

Kodinar, but the interior districts of Dhari and Khambha could not be supplied with such fodder in the absence of railway facilities.

28. Government did not receive as much assistance from private charity in Amreli as in Kadi; and, except in Damnagar, the Mahajans did not seem to be straining every nerve and spending their all in the attempt to preserve cattle. Indeed, there was no conspicuous display of private charity to relieve man or beast in the whole district. **Private charity.**

29. While I was at Kodinar I happened to ride by the Advi quarry, where there is an abundance of good building-stone. It struck me that it might command a good sale if it were transhipped to Bombay, Surat, or Broach by sea *viâ* the Velan port. Porebunder stone has a very good market in these large towns, and it seemed that the Kodinar stone should be able to compete advantageously with other Kathiawad quarries. A sum of 3000 rupees was sanctioned for the experiment of exporting building-stone to Baroda. I was told, however, that in the absence of any railway communication in Kodinar between Advi and Velan, the cost of conveyance would be enormous and would not pay. If the Velan port be improved and railways constructed in Amreli, Dhari, and Kodinar, the country might develop, and the stone industry in Kodinar in its turn receive a healthy impetus. **Advi stone quarry.**

30. Whenever during my tour I observed a village presenting a more than usually flourishing aspect, or showing fields covered with more prosperous crops than in my own territory, I used to inquire as to the cause of this. I often rode **Better irrigational facilities in some of the neighbouring villages.**

out quietly on purpose to observe the condition of such places, if they belonged to other Native States, and to compare it with the state of my own villages. I may cite an instance to the point. While at Damnagar I came across a village owned by the Dewan of Bhavnagar which looked very flourishing; and I also noticed on my way to Amreli that a village of the name of Matirala, not far from the Amreli frontier, belonging to the Thakore of Lathi, was actually smiling with plenty in the midst of the desolation surrounding it on all sides. I was much struck with this contrast, and I asked the Vahivatdar of Amreli to account for this difference in two villages so contiguously situated and so alike in the physical peculiarities of their soil and their climatic conditions. I instructed the Vahivatdar to go to the spot with a view to enable him to gather more accurate and detailed information, and also to teach him the wholesome lesson that it is never derogatory to the rank of any person to learn something good from another, be his rank ever so subordinate or low.

The report of the Vahivatdar confirmed the impression I had gathered before, that the Native States in Kathiawar generally took great pains to invest their money in the sinking of wells in their territories, thus conferring a sort of immunity from famine and scarcity on their agricultural classes. The prosperity of the villages noticed by me could be satisfactorily accounted for by the presence of such irrigational facilities. This observation serves to illustrate the marvellous effects of the feeling of property and proprietary interest. Arthur Young, the great political economist, has remarked: "Give a man a barren rock as his own property, and he will turn it into a smiling garden." And this wise maxim applies not only to estates but also to States. Where the intelligent owner feels that he has an hereditary interest in the soil he owns, he has an inducement to improve it. The belief that the ruler owns the soil in his kingdom is ingrained in the mind of the chief, and is the parent source of all improvements, which he feels it for his own interest to bestow on his property. Strip him of that belief, and his interest in the soil vanishes, degenerates into the mere temporary self-seeking greed of a hireling.

I may also mention that during my tours I used quietly to ride through the villages and see and estimate the value of the houses, wishing to get some idea of the material condition of the people. It struck me as very poor, though some of the better class of cultivators kept their homes very clean.

31. The outlying district of Okha was not included in the programme of my tour in Kathiawar; yet the question of relief in Okhamandal had, from the commencement, never failed to engage my serious attention. Here is a country that every third year falls a prey to visitations of drought and scarcity. It is a tract at once rocky and sterile, peopled by Waghers and other nomadic tribes, that mostly live on the product of their pastures and grazing-grounds. The fruit of agricultural industry is precarious, as it depends on the fitful movements of the clouds and the winds, and not on a regular

Okhamandal.

monsoon. Man, in such a country as Okha, fostered and spoiled by foreign interference, is as remote from the refining influence of civilisation and as averse from the love of honest toil as any spoiled child of Nature. It was, therefore, hard to tackle the problem of relief in Okha in a way which should afford satisfaction to both the helper and the helped.

In the year 1897, even though there was no real famine in Okha, it would seem that the authorities there spent more money on relief-works than probably was expended in some of the worst affected parts of British India. Even in ordinary good years the cost of the administration in Okhamandal is greater than the yield of the Taluka; and yet because, once, the people revolted against the Gaekwar, and he was unable without assistance to pacify the tract, the British Government has saddled upon him two British officers and the maintenance of a battalion. It seems as if this long-abiding consequence is out of all proportion to the slip of a moment. The effects of the Government order continue to burden an administration which is entirely different from that of the old rulers.

Relief-works in Okha.

32. Relief-works in Okha had been started since 1898, for the rainfall had been scanty over there, and the programme of useful relief-works had been well-nigh exhausted in that small territory even before the first three months of the present calamity had elapsed. Small tank-works and roads were provided in little villages, and the large number of men that flocked to them, owing to their close proximity to the different villages where the famine-stricken

lived, brought the programme to an end with an amazing rapidity. Work had yet to be provided for the people of Okha, backed up as these were by the Assistant Resident. Additional programmes of work were prepared, providing for more tracks in a district already interlaced with a network of roads which came into use only when, on rare occasions, inspecting State officials passed through the land. With the exception of the cut in the Gomati Creek, there was hardly any work in the programme that could be strictly justified by its necessity or utility. Some of the tanks and roads of negative utility, which made up the relief-works, had to be pushed through simply to provide the people of that lucky district with work and wages. The number of relief-seekers had gone up to nearly 50 per cent of the population of the province, and grave fears were entertained from the first that this costly system of work without return could not be long kept up without involving the State finances in inextricable muddle. To avoid this and yet to provide the people of Okha with means of support was a serious problem, the proposed solution of which was as follows :—

Tagavi for maintenance to the Waghers.

33. The Waghers, who, of the entire Okha population, formed the most difficult nut to crack, were the first to claim our attention. Some provision was to be made for them for their maintenance. Though not prevented by their social customs from doing so, the high ideas they were beginning to entertain of their own importance had the effect of rendering them unwilling to send their women to the

relief-works; and the wages their adult-males could earn on the works being hardly sufficient to maintain these last alone, left next to no surplus for the women and children. The system of relief-works was therefore not quite adapted to their social requirements. It was therefore proposed to make tagavi advances to the Waghers for their maintenance. The loan was to be a charge on their lands, and was made repayable by easy instalments, spread over a number of years. Under the peculiar tenure obtaining in Okhamandal the lands of the Waghers are inalienable beyond a certain limit, could not be attached or sold by judicial decrees, and could not be forfeited for default of payment of the fiscal dues. It was arranged through the Resident to remove this restriction, and the tagavi advanced to the Waghers was secured upon their lands. Recipients of this tagavi were thus rendered independent of relief-works, and were prohibited from resorting to them, with a view to reduce the number of relief-seekers on the Okha works.

Non-Waghers. Scheme of transporting them to distant places.

34. The non-Waghers were the next to claim our attention. The paucity of feasible schemes for Okha had rendered the problem of relief one of exceptional difficulty. It was thought that these non-Waghers, who were not so unruly or troublesome as their Wagher comrades, could without much difficulty be transported to Navsari or Baroda, where a number of useful works had been started, of which the completion was impossible owing to insufficient local numbers. Navsari had some useful items of work on its programme;

RELIEF-WORKS AT VISNAGAR

[Face page 67.

but as the district was not so badly off as the others, and as its agricultural population had been engaged in grass-cutting operations, it was thought impossible to finish them before the rains, unless large numbers of labourers were imported from abroad. To transport the non-Waghers to Navsari would result not only in providing them with the useful work, which was denied them in Okhamandal, but would also be conducive to the development of the Navsari district, which, in spite of its claims on our attention, was not receiving it, simply because its immediate necessities were less urgent than elsewhere. The scheme of transporting the non-Waghers would also have been useful as a distance test; for the really needy and sorely pinched would alone have elected to seek relief at such a distance from their own homes. There were difficulties in the execution of this scheme. The cost of transporting people to Navsari, and of sending them back at State expense at the approach of the rains, was prohibitive, and almost equalled the cost of maintaining them gratis for some months in their own homes. If the scheme had been carried out in the earlier stages of distress, it would have been worth our while to incur the expense; for then a larger interval of time before the advent of the monsoon would have afforded ampler scope for work, and the idea of getting other districts developed with the transported labour would have been thoroughly realised. As it was, the order to transport them to distant places, given in

November, was only taken up for execution in February, when the number of relief-works in Okha had been exhausted, and the time left for work in Navsari before the rains had become very short. The scheme, therefore, had to be dropped.

Tagavi to non-Waghers. *Del credere* system of agents.

35. The non-Waghers in Okhamandal had, however, to be fed and supported whether work was provided them or not. The number of relief-works was too limited to afford us the means of keeping them in work for any length of time. Tagavi had therefore to be given to these non-cultivating classes from amongst the non-Waghers. They had no lands on which the amount of tagavi could be charged, and it only remained for us to give these tagavi advances to them on personal security. The risk was necessarily great, and the following scheme was deemed worth a trial in order that some sort of security might be obtained. The Sar Subha was asked to consider the possibility of creating a sort of *del credere* agents. The Patels of the villages or the headmen of the various communities were to be asked to take up the position of such intermediaries, and on their recommendation and guarantee the State would lend tagavi to non-cultivators. The agents would be responsible to the State for the recovery of the money, but they would have the assistance of the State in recovering such dues; and in order to enlist their special interest in the concern, they would be given some commission on the sums recovered by them as a remuneration for their trouble and responsibility. If the agents had to pay the money, the State would undertake to assist them in the ultimate

realisation from the debtors, and would treat all such outstanding dues on the footing of unrecovered balances of Government dues. With the development of this system it was hoped that the project of lending tagavi for maintenance on the personal security of the debtors might be rendered practicable and its inherent difficulties minimised.

Conclusion.

36. Before I undertook to travel in my districts I had ordered (and I think that the order was published in the *Adnya-Patrika*) that no money was to be spent on celebrating my arrival at any place, and that no rayat was to make me a nazarana in accordance with old custom. Sometimes, however, a few well-to-do people insisted upon breaking this order. Under these circumstances, whenever any nazarana was made, I gave all the money to the relief of the poor. Not only did I do this, but, in order to inflict as little inconvenience as possible on the people for whose sole benefit my tours were undertaken, I took as few people and as little luggage with me as possible, so as to avoid the necessity of impressing labourers and carts. Now and again I personally saw these people paid by the officers and clerks. Finally, to give some expression to my feelings of sympathy for my countrymen, I also gave the workmen holidays, dinners, and extra wages.

Orders to collect information.

37. Before the famine made its appearance in an unmistakable manner, and before any relief-programmes were proposed to me, I had directed some of my officers, and specially those of the Survey Department, to collect certain statistical information about the state of existing wells.

Besides this, I had directed the survey officer to collate all suggestions for improvements made in the different survey settlement reports, so that I might be in a position to carry them out as far as possible, and so save the State from spending its resources on impromptu measures suggested at a time when something immediate had to be done. I was forced to resort to this and other devices, because the departments were quite unprepared with measures of utility. Later on I proposed and, systematically developed the extension of railway earthworks, which, if steadily pushed, would do much good to the country. I confess to a fondness for collecting useful information, and among other matters, had directed the compilation of various kinds of information, as, for instance, regarding the existing Annachhatra, etc., their nature, their scope, expenditure, etc. I wanted from this information to see whether we could utilise them for famine purposes without any hardship to anybody. I have subsequently impressed upon the officials concerned to have as many kinds of information as possible printed in such a form as may be most convenient for purposes of future reference.

BARODA CITY AND DIVISION

THE VADNAGAR ANNAGRUHA

[Face page 73.

III.—BARODA CITY AND DIVISION

1. After my return from the Amreli district, I stayed for some weeks at the capital before I set out on a tour through the Baroda division, for the purpose of observing the condition of the people and the progress of the relief-works. Large numbers of famine-stricken people from the various divisions of the State had sought refuge in the city, which seemed also to have attracted a crowd of persons in search of relief from other Native States and from adjoining British tracts. Their condition was very pitiable, and the problem of devising means to alleviate their sufferings had caused us much anxiety. Fears were rightly entertained that, as the season advanced and the hot weather approached, the distress caused by the terrible drought would reach a climax, so that the administration would have to strain every nerve to cope with a calamity which was fast assuming a grave aspect and unmanageable dimensions. Baroda district.

Happily there was no dearth of great and useful works in this division, and our difficulties were much lightened by the adequate number of remunerative projects that had been devised for the employment of relief-labour.

2. While I was travelling in the Amreli division, I had asked for information from the Programme of works in Baroda.

Minister and the Accountant-General as to the likelihood of a probable increase in the number of relief-seekers and in the cost of maintaining them, as the famine increased in intensity. When this was ascertained, I set myself to the task of getting the programmes of the different divisions settled, as I was anxious to provide for even a larger number of works than could possibly be required in the future. I had impressed upon the officials the advisability of suggesting schemes which would suffice for full six months after the necessity for affording relief had ceased. I must in this connection pay a tribute to the valuable work done by the Minister throughout this trying ordeal. His large sympathy and experience in the arrangement of famine programmes deserve high praise. I should also thank the Accountant-General for the ability and quickness with which he made out the necessary calculations.

At first the Baroda division was not better off than the others as regards the number of useful works which could be undertaken for purposes of relief, and I had actually to hunt out big useful works for the division. In course of time, however, the programme was made to include several large works of great utility. Its items comprised railway earthworks, irrigational and drainage schemes, large tanks, and some necessary roads. There were two or three metal-breaking works also at the different quarries. The Baroda-Godhra loop-line and the extension of the Petlad railway to the boundary of the Raj towards Cambay had been sanctioned in the earlier months, and large numbers of people in their neighbourhood had sought work at these centres. The Public Works Department had been asked to align and lay out the Miyagam-Sinore, the Bahadurpur-Songir, and the Padra-Mobhe lines, so as to enable us to take them up whenever the necessities of famine-relief should require us to do so. Instructions were also given to keep in readiness schemes for the Nariad-Sojitra loop-line and the Waghodia-Savli railway, in order to provide for all possible demands for work. Some of these lines I had myself to suggest on the spur of the moment, as I found that the department was fumbling about in search of large useful works. I thought of undertaking some of these lines merely to provide a sufficient number of works, though I doubted from the first whether they would be of a paying nature.

Large amounts had been sanctioned for the Karamsad and Sandesar drains, which would serve the needs of the territories lying contiguous to British territory and the Cambay State. The Karachia and the Haripura tanks, which had been suggested by the Subha, Mr. Khaserav, besides being useful undertakings, were especially needed to meet the requirements of the Bhils and Kolis who abound in that part of the district.

In one of my rides to Ajwa, a couple of men from the Taluka had told me that the Bhils were slaughtering cows and buffaloes for want of any other occupation. On inquiry I learned that a number of small relief-works was in progress in that part of the district, and that a big scheme was being prepared for it. I asked the Subha to hasten its completion. I always encourage suggestions from whatever quarter they may come, and make use of them, after duly weighing their chances of success. The Subha had told me that a quarry at a certain place in the district should perhaps be explored. I sent my Chief Engineer, Mr. Graham Lynn, to examine the site and report on it. Before his opinion had come, as I was anxious to provide a sufficient number of works, I sanctioned the expenditure of a sum of money to defray the cost of ascertaining the quality of the quarry, and the Chief Engineer was empowered to stop work if he thought that the money would be wasted.

Besides the works I have mentioned, there was the Vishwamitri feeder scheme for a reservoir at Asoj. Originally there were two schemes in connection with this undertaking, prepared several years back, printed under my orders, and kept ready for future use, whenever the necessity might arise. One was to excavate a large irrigational tank at Asoj, which would also be useful in supplementing the water-supply of the capital; and the other was merely to construct a feeder canal to the Ajwa lake. Neither of these schemes was absolutely required at the time.

But as I was anxious to extend the programme, I was compelled, as it were, by the necessities of the situation to sanction the feeder project. The alternative of a big irrigation reservoir had to be abandoned, as I was advised that an irrigation lake in that locality would not be profitable. In other words, the people would refuse to pay for the use of the water. In Native States this theory of consent on the part of the subjects is at times carried so far, that Government is hampered in its desire to undertake large and useful works. The people have lost their old theories of government, and many of them do not know what the modern theories are. They attempt to imitate the British, but the indelible marks of their own character remain. Sometimes they fail so completely in their attempt to copy a foreign and ill-understood model, that it would be better if they trusted to their own strong common-sense.

I had another object in placing the Asoj feeder work on the programme, even though expert opinion was far from being sanguine as to its utility for purposes of irrigation. I had long thought of importing into Baroda and Navsari batches of workmen from Amreli and Okhamandal, where the programme of remunerative works was meagre, and was reported to be rapidly running out. I consequently gave orders to bring several groups of workmen from Amreli and employ them on the Vishwamitri cut, and had several times to insist upon the execution of my orders.

The most important irrigational undertaking in this district was the Orsang canal work at Jhojwa, which was calculated to supply water to fields for a length of about thirty miles, and to cost about a million of rupees. With the insertion of this work in the local programme, much of my anxiety lest we should fail to find new useful works for the division was removed.

Visits to relief-works in the city.

3. As mentioned above, large numbers of vagrants had flocked to the town in the hope of obtaining some relief-work, or, rather, in that of living at large upon the charity of others. I

am told that many of these people preferred to starve rather than resort to relief-works, though they did not mind going there if they could get their food for nothing. They disliked the poor-house, because their liberty was restricted, and what they preferred was to get their food there and to stroll about begging in the streets. It was a curious sight to see strings of poor people entering the city in the early morning with loads of fuel and bundles of faggots on their heads, and this only a few days after the drought had unmistakably set in. These loads of firewood they had to sell at very cheap rates to earn some means of livelihood. Grass had become scarce, and a number of people from the surrounding villages came to the city to sell, at fancy prices, what looked like dirt and weeds, but was termed by them grass. However, even such means of earning a livelihood soon failed, and no other course was left to these poor people but to resort to the relief-works opened in the city. To find employment for these wandering refugees some useful works, calculated to improve the appearance and the sanitation of the city, were started,—the filling up of the Bhimnath and the Madan Talavs (tanks), the improvement of the sites near the Dufferin Hospital and the Bagikhana (the State carriage-house), the deepening of the tank near the elephant-stables, the repair of the Akota causeway, and the Padra road. At the suggestion of the Minister, I directed a large number of these undertakings to be started in order to check the begging that was going on.

I ordered many of the stragglers in the city to be located in particular places under the surveillance of the police, who were directed to prevent them, except within special hours, from strolling about the streets. I had constantly to repeat this order at different stages of the famine season, and to insist upon its proper fulfilment.

People often complain of zulum in a Native State, and those who are ignorant, or pretend to be so, often take it for granted that zulum exists ; but to my limited experience it appears that any severe order passed in a Native State, even though it be just, is seldom strictly carried out. I simply state the fact, and refrain from all explanations.

Long before my regular tours had commenced, I had paid several visits to the works that were being carried on in the city of Baroda, and to the famine and other hospitals there and in its neighbourhood. Some of these remarks, therefore, ought chronologically to appear elsewhere ; but for the sake of convenience they have been grouped here.

In course of time the number of relief-seekers on the Bhimnath work, which was going up by leaps and bounds, became too large, and somewhat unmanageable. There was such a great concourse of workmen by the side of the station road, that the carriage traffic there was hampered, and pedestrians were inconvenienced. People from other works in the city flocked to the Bhimnath camp, and helped to swell the numbers.

It was said that the piece-work system which was enforced on the Godhra loop-line was not relished by the workmen, who were also discontented with the wages they earned. I had, therefore, to modify the system to some extent.

The system of work enforced on the Bhimnath tank was apparently the more attractive. I directed the Minister to inquire into the cause of this disparity of numbers on the different works, and to get the great crowds on the Bhimnath work reduced to manageable proportions.

At Bhimnath the Municipality was carrying on the work at a very expensive rate. I believe it was something more than one rupee per every hundred cubic feet, while the rate in ordinary times would be only six annas. On being questioned why the work was so costly, an important officer in charge of the work told me that they understood that the object of Government was, not to look to expenditure or to the genuineness of work, but merely to pay the people under the pretext of making them do something. I asked him to shift the place of excavation, and to employ the wheeled trucks and rails which were lying idle in large quantities at a certain place near the capital. I explained to him that the object of Government was certainly to protect the people, but at the same time to get as much useful work done as was possible under the circumstances. I suggested plenty of other works which the city was badly in need of.

The result of the order to open many works was that a number of people from other places came to them, because, owing to certain facilities and attractions in the town, people preferred to work there rather than at a distance. Again, several departments were engaged in carrying out these works, and therefore the systems varied, while the knowledge of the code was practically *nil.* The answers of the officers on the various works to inquiries, made with a view to ascertain if there was any uniformity of system, indicated rather the existence of discrepancies. So I directed the Minister to reduce the aggregate number of people on the city relief-works as far as the necessities of the situation might warrant his doing so.

Other relief measures.

4. (*a*) Besides affording relief on these works, I had sanctioned the advance of large sums as tagavi to cultivators in order to enable them to sink new wells, and thus to impart to their fields some immunity from the recurrence of scarcity and famine. Further amounts were also sanctioned to provide tagavi for the purchase of seed and of agricultural implements required by the cultivators.

(*b*) I directed an orphanage to be opened at Baroda, where the Subha was instructed to maintain all orphans of tender years and children deserted by their parents in these times of dire distress and widespread suffering.

(*c*) Cheap grain-shops, maintained by the charity of private individuals and by the contribution of the Khangi Department, were opened at convenient places in the town, where the indigent section of the population could buy articles of food at reduced prices.

(*d*) Orders had also been issued to grant scarcity allowances to all servants of the State, civil and military, whose monthly salaries did not exceed 12 rupees; while the usual deductions made on the salaries of the military employees of the State for uniform, accoutrements, and horses, were suspended. An extension of this order was afterwards by logical sequence asked by and granted to some of the village servants at first excluded.

(*e*) As an experiment, too, permission was granted to maintain a cattle camp at Harni near Baroda. From the very first I was inclined to think that the plan would ultimately turn out a failure, and the event has proved that my fears were not unreasonable. I had my doubts as to the validity of the securities offered to obtain the nucleus of the capital required for this camp, and was, therefore, not disposed to accept too easily the recommendations of the officers who favoured the plan.

It is hard to come across continuity of interest and energy. Perhaps because I have been brought into closer contact with our own people than with others, I have observed this defect to a special degree in them. This lamentable shortcoming is, in my opinion, partly due to the absence of proper education, to ignorance of high ideals, such as the pleasure of duty performed; but it is also the fault of indifferent and apathetic Governments, whose standard of reward for merit has been varied and uncertain, while they have sometimes refused the subject races any kind of encouragement. This is to be deplored, and every attempt must be made to set our policy right, though I know from certain experience that I am speaking of a fight against almost overpowering odds.

Even in their ideas of method and system, a difference can be seen between officers who have travelled and those who have never gone abroad.

5. My attention had early been drawn to

CATTLE CAMP

[Face page 82.

the systems of assigning work to and exacting it from the different groups of labourers. We had to be very careful to see that, on the one hand, too stringent tasks were not imposed on the workmen, and that, on the other, something like a proportionate out-turn of work was secured in return. A famine administration, in order to be successful, requires to combine leniency with due economy, consideration with discrimination, and generosity with justice. Without the union of the one and the other, it has the tendency to degenerate into squeamish parsimony or lavish prodigality. Modes of exacting work.

The system in vogue in many of the affected districts was one of exacting task-work from gangs of labourers who worked either individually or in family groups. The work turned out by each gang was measured at the end of the day, and wages were paid according to the regulations of the famine code. The scales of tasks and wages provided by the code were not necessarily in commensurate proportion; for the work exacted was regulated by the average physical capacity of a labourer in a season of distress and by the nature of the material on which he had to work, while the scale of wages, which were payable either in kind or in a money equivalent, was fixed by the physical needs of the labourer according to age and sex. Task-work system.

One consequence of this task-work system was that the labourers had to be classified into different grades according to their physical fitness, and the task imposed on each class was once for all determined and provided for in the code. The wages, however, not having any exact pro- Disadvantages.

portion to the quantity of work done, did not fall or rise in proportion to the out-turn, but were rigidly fixed according as the labourer was a man or a woman, an adult or a child. A labourer in the first class, for instance, had to turn out a greater quantity of work than his fellow-labourer in the second class, but the wages to which the former was entitled did not exceed those of the latter in the same proportion. There was thus no adequate inducement for a man to work to the utmost of his capacity; he could afford with impunity to be degraded to the lower class, as this saved him the trouble of turning out the full tale of work. The code, no doubt, provided for the imposition of fines in cases of wilful negligence or laziness; but the line of separation between laziness and physical unfitness could not always be sharply drawn, and there was no guarantee that the low-paid subordinates, who had practically to carry out the system, would always use discrimination in distinguishing between cases. There was the likelihood of the supervisors treating every case as one of pretended illness, and thus stinting the relief where it was urgently needed; or of their interpreting every case as one of real inability, and thus squandering the resources of the State.

Minimum wages.

Besides this, the code provided for the payment of minimum wages to every labourer, and even the imposition of fines was limited by this minimum wage, which was fixed according to the lowest estimate of the physical wants of a man.

The full wages to be earned by honest work were not, as mentioned above, proportionate to the full quantity of work, and thus a labourer, secure of his minimum wage, had no stimulus to turn out a greater quantity of work. Malingering on a large scale was, consequently, one result of the system in vogue on the famine-works. The Government spent large amounts of money in affording relief; but the work turned out fell far short of the quantity one had a reasonable right to expect even in those dire times.

Another inconvenience of the task-work system.

6. Another difficulty in the working out of the system was that it necessitated the classifying of labourers into several grades, for each of which a different quantity of work was assigned by the code. Labourers in one class were all entitled to the same wages, even though some of them might have turned out a good deal more work than the task fixed for their class, and yet not quite sufficient to entitle them to the wages of the class above theirs. Having no inducement, therefore, to work even a bit more than the minimum quantity imposed by the task, there was no likelihood of their exerting themselves to the utmost. Besides, the classification was itself artificial, and involved too many nice distinctions, to which it was not always possible for the subordinate officers rigidly to adhere.

The danger of leaving too much to the discretion of petty officials was always great, and to avoid it a complicated and costly machinery had to be employed for effective supervision.

Advantages.

The task system with the fixed minimum wage had its good side, for it savoured less of the contract system of hiring and enforcing labour, and it left more play for the generous and sympathetic instincts, which were so much needed in those times; yet from an economic and administrative point of view it left much to be desired, especially with regard to the proper adjustment of details.

Piece-work system.

7. The other system of exacting work may be styled the piece-work system, according to which a measured piece of work is allotted to a group of workmen, which they may finish as best they can, their wages, regulated by the quantity of work turned out, being paid to the group on the completion of the assigned piece. Such groups are very often made up of people belonging to one and the same family, or of persons who undertake to co-operate and consequently work peaceably together. The wages are paid to the head of the gang, who distributes them to each of the members according to previous agreement.

Advantages.

The advantages of this system are manifold :

(1) It secures adequate inducement for honest work by providing wages proportionate to the out-turn of work.

(2) It does away with the necessity of complicated classification and lessens the task of supervision. The work turned out each day has not to be measured to see whether the individual daily task has been effected or not. A piece is measured out at starting, and needs no re-examination till it is completed.

(3) By removing the guarantee of the minimum wage it impels a man to put forth all his energies; and, by providing wages proportionate to any aliquot part of the work done, it creates a desire to work even a fraction more, and so to earn the corresponding increase of wage.

8. Against these advantages one drawback in

the piece-work system may be pointed out. As it more closely resembles the ordinary process of getting work done by contract, it seems to be out of place in a famine administration, which undertakes works not so much for their intrinsic worth as to provide means for subsistence to the indigent during a season of trial. Disadvantage.

The wages being regulated by the quantity of work done, those who are really out of condition have no sure means of subsistence, as they are not likely to be accepted by any co-operative group of labourers. Unless, therefore, some further safeguards are provided for the really needy, the piece-work system would fail to afford relief to those most in need of help.

9. The question as to which of the two systems discussed above could with advantage be uniformly adopted on all the relief-works in the State came up to me for decision after my return from the Kadi and Amreli trips. I had also to revise the scale of the minimum wage, which, as pointed out before, owing to its being quite sufficient for the ordinary wants of the poor, failed to provide any stimulus for greater exertion on their part. Reduction in the minimum wage.

My idea was to distinguish those who were really incapable of working from those who were only lazy and malingering, and to mete out different treatment to them. If the minimum ration were reduced to a point a little below the quantity absolutely required for subsistence, it would make the indolent just feel the pinch of real want and induce them to work with greater energy, so as to enable them to earn more for their livelihood. For those who were really disabled by weakness the minimum wage was not to be reduced at all. On the contrary, I thought that the minimum in their case should be still further raised so that they might regain a state of physical fitness. A system which combined indulgent treatment for those who really stood in need of help with a little rigour and stringency towards those who only made a feint of incapacity appeared to me very preferable to one uniform system of a minimum wage for all alike.

Padra and Dabka.

10. In October 1899, when all hope of an improvement taking place in the season had been abandoned, and just as the famine was setting in, I visited Padra and Dabka, where the relief-operations were being organised. I inquired of the Patel of Dabka as to the condition of the people in his village, and I learnt from him that several among them had deserted their homes and gone away from the village, some to seek work at the capital, and some to Malwa, where they thought the rains had been more favourable than in their own province. I may here remark that the expressions, "they had deserted their homes," "they had gone away after locking up their houses," and other such phrases, do not mean that the people had left their homes for good with no intention of returning to them, as is sometimes supposed by people who are not acquainted with the ways and modes of expression used amongst country-folk.

The population of this district consists chiefly of Kolis, Machis (fishermen), and other non-cultivating classes. I wondered what works could be started for such folk in their own villages. The Subha had an idea of constructing a small tank either in, or near, the ravines there, but I sanctioned certain other works, which I have no doubt must have met the wants of those who could not leave Dabka in search of relief elsewhere, either at Baroda, Padra, or Petlad.

Further tagavi for Padra.

11. (*a*) At Padra the people requested me to open some large works for the district. I had a long conversation with the local Vahivatdar, and asked him what use he had made of the amount at his disposal for tagavi advances. I was informed that the whole sum had been spent, and that further sums were absolutely necessary for the people in his district. The Vahivatdar told me that he had applied to the Sar Subha for more money, but that he had up to that moment received no reply. I had a talk with the Naib Subha and a few other prominent men of the place on the same and kindred subjects. The cultivators expressed the hope that no revenue would be collected for the year, as they had only the indulgence of Government, whom they regarded in the light of their Mábáp (parent), to fall back upon! I sanctioned on the spot a sum of 15,000 rupees for further tagavi grants in the Padra district, and asked my secretary to inform the Sar Subha of the order. It is not possible for the State to meet every demand for tagavi, as very frequently the sums asked for in advance are so large as to cover the rent of the holding for an indefinite number of years.

(*b*) As I went along the road, I noticed that at several places people had sunk new wells and were employed in watering their fields. The

Condition of the people in the Padra district.

crops reared under this irrigation had grown up here and there, but the number of the wells newly sunk by the people struck me as much too low. I inquired as to the reasons of this inadequate number, and also sought information regarding the use the people had made of the tagavi advanced to them. The Vahivatdar, who is an intelligent and steady officer, told me that in several parts of his district no wells could be sunk with advantage, as the water found in them was brackish and consequently useless for purposes of irrigation. I was also told that a certain number of new wells was being sunk, while some old ones were being repaired and brought into actual use.

I observed that, owing to the extreme difficulty of procuring fodder for the cattle, the leaves of the trees were being removed and utilised. The peasant women, their short frocks fastened tightly round their loins and tied across their shoulders, were here and there to be seen perched on the branches of the trees and engaged in lopping off the leaves. It was a sad sight to see long avenues of noble trees thus denuded of their foliage. I made inquiries of the cultivators as to whether the feeding of their cattle upon mango and other leaves had any prejudicial effect upon their health. Opinions were divided on the point, but a great majority thought that it did no great harm.

I could not prolong my stay at Dabka, as the grass sent for my horses from Baroda was running short, and there was much difficulty in collecting more in the neighbourhood without inflicting hardship on the people.

12. In the second week of March I proceeded to Petlad to inspect the progress of the relief-operations there. There were two main works in that district, viz. the Petlad-Cambay railway and the Karamsad drain. Petlad is a prosperous town and has lands which, in normal years, are very fertile. Its population consists of several respectable classes, and of well-to-do Patidars. I was surprised to see that the condition of the labourers on the works was not bad, and that their number was small, and almost entirely limited to the lower classes of society. I naturally asked what happened to the poor Patidars in this season of general distress, and was told that the old social sentiment, which prevented almost all, and particularly the respectable sections of our community, from resorting to relief-works, was still strongly prevalent amongst them. Besides this, it must be borne in mind that the Petlad folk are better off than people of other parts of the division. The Patidars of the town are industrious, intelligent, thrifty, and of a calculating turn of mind. Naturally, therefore, they were, to some extent, better able to stand the stress of the times. Petlad.

However, with a view to prevent their suffering any undue hardship from an exaggerated sense of self-respect, I directed the giving of tagavi advances to them on certain conditions.

I visited the earthworks of the Petlad-Cambay railway that were being laid down at some distance from the town. I had asked my secretary to accompany me in order to make a thorough inquiry into the complaints of the Petlad-Cambay railway.

workmen, and to examine the system of accounts followed there. I heard a few of the labourers grumbling about the heavy work exacted from them, and the inadequacy of the wages paid to them on the work. This reminded me of similar complaints I had heard in other divisions.

Karamsad drain.

The work of excavating the Karamsad drain was also progressing at some distance from Petlad. One day I rode out early in the morning and proceeded slowly towards the work.

The number of workmen here was reported to be very small; but this could be accounted for in various ways. I have already said that the general level of wellbeing in this district was high, and that there was an old-fashioned dislike to resorting to the relief-works. But, in addition to this, I observed that many of the landholders were, with the help of labourers, engaged in rearing crops by means of irrigation from the wells they had newly sunk or repaired, and were thus kept off the relief-works. Lastly, the piece-work system, which was being enforced on this work, might have in a certain measure helped the various causes mentioned above in preventing the numbers from assuming large proportions.

Proceeding, as I say, leisurely towards this work, I visited several villages on the road. During the course of one of my conversations with the Dheds whom I met on the way, and who seemed to be in fair condition, I heard them complaining of want of work. I asked them what steps they had taken to find it. They told me they had repaired to a certain work, where they were refused admission. I subsequently learnt that they had gone to a non-Gaekwari work, from whence they had to return. I then asked them why they did not make a second attempt, and whether they were aware of the railway work that was going on near Petlad. They said they were not. The ignorance and helplessness of these men struck me, and I asked the Patel to draft them on to the railway work. I afterwards learnt that the Public Works authorities discouraged the admission to that work of labourers who were not able to turn out a sufficient amount of work, but these Dheds were, I think, physically fit to do the required quantity, and were not likely to be refused admission on that ground.

After hearing the complaints of the Dheds, I asked the Sar Subha, Mr. Dhamnaskar, a very conscientious and trustworthy officer, and my secretary, Mr. Yusufalli, to sift the whole matter and submit their report to me. I discussed the conclusions they arrived at in their report with several of the Public Works officers, and one result of these deliberations was that I instantly issued orders to grant higher remuneration to the workmen, and to open another small work at a convenient distance from the main work, where provision could be made for the weak and the disabled.

During my stay here I frequently went out riding or walking, and weighed the comparative condition of the villages, the people, the cattle. I often talked with the inhabitants, as well as with folk from British villages. Once or twice they represented their condition as very grave, but, happily, their complaints turned out to be not quite true. The men who gave me these exaggerated accounts of the condition of their village proved on inquiry to be interested parties, who had something to gain by making misrepresentations. They were British subjects who had either lands or some other monetary interests in a Baroda village. The village about which they had complained was mostly inhabited by Mohammedans. I sent my secretary, Mr. Yusufalli, to inquire into their allegations. It is always a custom with me to send different officers in different directions to examine different works. It is partly done to achieve the largest possible amount of work in the minimum of time.

Gratuitous relief.

13. I had for some time observed that the poor people of the Baroda division presented a very emaciated look, and this set me to work to try and discover the causes of this somewhat premature physical prostration. Why the condition of the people in the Baroda division should have grown so bad in so short a time excited my curiosity. Some told me that people from the Mahi Kantha and the neighbouring foreign districts, who had nothing to live upon, had come there; others attributed it to the fact that the worst cases of famine-stricken folk had assembled in the capital. Such were the reasons to which the apparent condition of the people was generally ascribed. From the reports I heard at Petlad, I at once directed a poor-house to be opened in the city.

I had already sanctioned the amount of one

hundred thousand rupees, or more, from the Khangi for the distribution of gratuitous relief in poor-houses and kitchens, and by the time I returned from Petlad, this order was made applicable to the whole State. I may here remark, *en passant*, that kitchens had been started long before this in the capital, where the physical condition of the people had excited attention. The infants, the aged, the infirm, and the destitute were thus provided with means of subsistence in these asylums. The order served to supplement one shortcoming of the system, which had not made adequate provision for the disabled and the decrepit on the relief-works.

Limited piece-work system.

14. I had learnt from a conversation with one of my officers, some days before, that a previous order about the piece-work system had not been properly interpreted, and that it required to be amplified to some extent. This, with the additional light thrown on it by the experience acquired in Petlad, led me to pass my final orders on the subject, by which the system was modified to some extent. They were the outcome of a meeting which gave rise to a good deal of hot discussion and argument, followed by a regular count of votes. According to this modified system, all the intricacies of complicated classification were once for all done away with, the labourers being divided into two groups only, consisting of (1) those who were in fair health and were fit for work, and (2) those who were physically unfit. Work was to be allotted according to the piece system only to labourers of the first class, and the wages to be paid to them for a certain quantity of

work were to be fixed at reasonable rates. The average working capacity of such groups of labourers was to be carefully observed in numerous instances, and the wages to be paid for the whole piece were to be so fixed as to leave at least one pound and a quarter of grain to those amongst them who, in spite of honest endeavour, were able to turn out comparatively little work. Those who were not disposed to shirk work could thus make sure of obtaining at least a minimum wage sufficient for subsistence. Below this level their wage would not be allowed to decline. I was inclined to have no maximum limit fixed at all, but gave way to the serious representations of officers in the interests of finance. It is a question whether my view should not be carried out when the famine code comes to be revised. If it is found impossible to give effect to my recommendation, I would suggest that the maximum limit of the rations of almost all classes of labourers should be increased by at least half a pound more. I have ordered every officer to watch the defects of the present code, and to correct them before they prove mischievous. Ultimately, I intend to have these suggestions collected, so that they may be of use in correcting the code where it is found necessary to do so.

I always like to study the application of an order and to encourage others to do the same. What success this habit of mine has met with need not be stated here. To me administration is a science, and, studied properly, it is a very engaging pursuit, which throws open a wide door to the study of human nature.

15. To avert the evils of a guaranteed

minimum to which I have adverted, it was also arranged that those of the labourers who had, in the first instance, been classed in the first group of physically fit, and yet were unable to earn even the minimum quantity of one pound and a quarter of grain, should be placed under medical observation for some time. If it appeared during such period that they were only malingering, that they were really in a state of tolerable fitness, that they could work harder if they were only so inclined, they were to be kept on a penal ration of one pound only per day. The object of thus diminishing the minimum provided for by the code was to make them feel that they were liable to be debarred from even the minimum of subsistence, to make them feel the pinch of want, and thus to compel them to exert themselves. If, on the other hand, they were certified by the medical officer in charge to be really debilitated, they were at once to be removed from the able-bodied category and placed in the second class of the physically unfit; their rations were to be increased from the penal amount of one pound to the minimum scale of a pound and a quarter, as provided by the code. The medical officers were also cautioned not to prolong the period of observation of ordinary cases beyond two or three weeks, so as to avoid the danger of further enfeebling those who were really weak by keeping them too long on penal rations. Penal ration.

16. Those who were pronounced to be physically incapacitated for work under the piece system were to be classed in the second group, and work of a light nature was to be Light work to the weak.

imposed on them. They were to be given the minimum wage, as provided for by the code. Those of them who were too reduced even to do a light task were to be treated as patients in the hospital, and were to be given more food than was provided for them by the code. After they had fully regained their health, they were again to be treated as ordinary labourers.

Aliens on the relief-works of the State.

17. I had great difficulty in prevailing upon the Minister to send back from the works people who had come there from British territory. He did not like to do it, he said, as the measure was discountenanced by the report of the last Famine Commission. Subsequently reports published in the newspapers and coming from other sources convinced him of the fact that the British Government were doing the same thing with foreigners on their works, and were taking action to send them away. The Minister, however, was not even then prepared to budge from the position he had assumed. The subordinate officers under him also showed signs of fear and hesitation in carrying out my orders to send back foreigners to British territories. I believe they feared lest they might thereby incur the displeasure of the British Government, though they would by no means acknowledge the fact.

Visit to the poorhouse.

18. After my return to the capital in April I visited the poorhouse to inspect the condition of its inmates and to examine its internal arrangements. I was much struck with the wretched condition and the dirty looks of most of its inmates. Some of them seem to have been reduced to the condition of mere skeletons.

INMATES OF VADNAGAR ANNAGRUHA

[Face page 98.

The young children especially, with swarms of flies pestering them and buzzing about their dirty persons, excited my greatest compassion. Their eyes had sunk into their sockets, and they scarcely possessed clothes wherewith to cover their framework of bones. I made minute inquiries into the nature of the food and the quantity given to the different inmates, the mode in which it was cooked for them, and the pots and utensils given to them to eat out of. I noticed some defects in the details of the system, and suggested certain improvements. I recommended the officers to try a change of diet. Under the provisions of the code, rice and dal (pulse) were given to the inmates of poorhouses, while most of them preferred to have bajri (millet) and other kinds of grain, and some in their enervated condition could not even digest their portion of rice and dal. I ordered the requisite change of diet to be made in this as in all poorhouses, and I hope the Minister has carried out my directions in good time. When the Famine Code of the State is revised, this suggestion as to a change of diet should, I think, be incorporated into its modified provisions. I would also recommend that the revised code should contain some provision for supplying clothing to the inmates of poorhouses. I drew the attention of the managing authorities to the dirty and slovenly appearance of these miserable folk, and asked the officers to see that greater facilities for bathing at regular intervals were provided. A word of acknowledgment is due to Messrs. Avate and Dharnidhar for the great pains they took in managing this poorhouse.

Without much expense, a great deal of cleanliness, tidiness, and regularity can be introduced into the internal management of the poorhouses. But to carry out these small but important details men are wanted who will closely look after the management, and, above all, men who have experienced a better mode of life than falls to the lot of many people in our country, who are too often born and bred up in slovenliness. Their action in the management of a poorhouse is only a reflex of their own minds, which are in constant contact with too low a level of civilisation.

Certain defects which we find in the management of the poorhouses are found in the houses of the managers themselves. If they are wanting in earnestness and sympathy and in high aspirations to mitigate the sufferings of their fellow-men, it is because their own interests have never been properly looked after. They have from the commencement been strangers to sympathetic treatment, and every high and ennobling ambition has been crushed out of them. They have had no share in, they have not even witnessed, the award of punishment on the one hand to such as have misbehaved, or of reward on the other to such as have been philanthropic.

Orphanage. 19. Before my visit to the poorhouse I had inspected the orphanage, or rather the asylum for young deserted children. I jotted down some information about many of the boys maintained there, from which I found that a large number of them were no orphans, but had parents who had renounced the obligation of supporting them, and had left them there under false pretences, in order that they might thus avail themselves of Government aid.

Both the poorhouse and the orphanage were to some extent subsidised by private enterprise and philanthropy; and a word of praise is surely due to those who put into practice their feelings of sympathy.

Sankheda Orsang irrigation work.

20. As already mentioned, the Orsang irrigation project was one of the most important relief-works in the programme for the Baroda division. The scheme having been approved by expert opinion, I accorded my sanction to it in the month of April. After my return to the capital from Navsari and Lanowli, in the early part of May, I was requested to lay the foundation-stone of the dam on the Orsang river near Jhojwa.

I did so, and the speech I made on the occasion indicated my views on the famine-relief policy; it is given at the end of the notes on my tour in the Navsari district, at the conclusion of this book.

Dabhoi

Invitation.

21. On my way back from Jhojwa, I was requested by the local officials and Mahajans of Dabhoi to visit the asylum for the poor there established. I accepted their invitation, though I was hard pressed for time.

The foundation of asylum.

22. The poorhouse had been brought into existence by the charity of the local officials and the benevolent Mahajans of the place.

Government also contributed something towards the expenses of the institution. The Mahajans and the local officials took great trouble in its management. For all this the official and non-official members of the community deserve a hearty recognition.

Fortifications.

23. As I neared the town of Dabhoi I looked out of my carriage and saw the massive stone walls of the town, so interesting from an historical and archæological point of view. The sight of these fortifications could not fail to force back my mind to pictures of the past.

My thoughts.

24. I thought of the old times in which labour was cheap and living was plentiful when the season was favourable. Many had to die of hunger and thirst where nature had proved unkind; but perhaps the hardship was softened by greater benevolence than exists now, when the conflict between different interests is more prominent, and disintegrating influences in the community are more powerful. Exportation was then difficult, and surplus produce was stored up and often allowed to rot. The present admirable organisation of famine-administration was conspicuous by its absence; the motive force to help the proletariat in the old times may perhaps have been different.

Could these dilapidated walls speak out all the memories they keep stored in their crumbling masses of stone, how the bare outlines of history would be filled in with living detail and romantic story! What a panorama connects itself with these old and historic Indian cities! What memories of the old Hindu Raj that existed here about A.D. 1100, its encouragement of arts and industry, its patronage of military courage and ability, its picturesque and motley crowd of retainers! What animated pictures of the proud, brave, fanatic, and iconoclastic Mohammedans, and of the brief supremacy of the Maratha nation, too brief for the constructive genius of the race in the art of government to manifest itself! Within these ramparts what scenes of tumult, caste-jealousies, civil wars, deaths and burials, gay scenes, marriages, processions, and births, had palpitated across the human scene, and left their echoes in these great stones, silent now to the busy and harassed workers of a later century, or suggesting only vain dreams to one who is passing through a stricken country from centre of suffering to centre of suffering!

That past glory serves only to shed a more gloomy light on the present. The barracks of stone were once reserved for the bearers of arms; now they are used for the improvident and the famine-stricken.

Description of the day and the country.

25. But these vain imaginings had to cease with the slowing down of the small train at my destination. Their dreamy imaginations made the old Hindus neglect too much their material interest, and we to-day have to face stern and sordid realities. It is difficult to describe the desolation of that scene. A day hushed and heat-stricken, without breath of wind, motion of leaf, or flight or chirping of birds, or the sight of any animal; not even the circling of the kite in the blue wideness of the heavens! The city was void of any throng of men, nor was there the sound of any bell from

its temples. There was a pervading and appalling air of silence, an air of universal affliction and silent fear of the anger of Heaven made visible in that burning sun and those long-rainless skies; this sun which seemed to have deposed the other elements of nature and usurped sole sovereignty, tiring man and beast with the tyranny of his rays. Earth itself lay parched, bare, and prostrate; no longer a pregnant mother of life and nurse of men, but herself thirsting for water, herself stricken with famine. No blade of grass, no trace of crop; the country lay wide, bare, and brown! Trees and cactus alone seemed to defy the burning rays!

Visit to asylum.

26. I was escorted by a few well-dressed citizens to view the famine-stricken inmates of an asylum that was not far off from the station. Under the temporary sheds I saw about a hundred or two hundred persons, mostly women and children. They were reduced to terrible extremity; they were mere bags of bones; their skin had a wrinkled and unhealthy appearance; their eyes were sunken in and lacked lustre; some of them had inflamed eyes, with so much mucus that swarms of flies had mustered round them, and pestered these unfortunates. They were so feeble that they had hardly the strength to drive them away. They sat almost motionless and took but passing notice of the visitors. They did not say a word, but showed respect and gratitude only by greater silence than usual. They would have lifted up their hands and blessed their benefactors; but they had no strength to do it. They would have covered

A GROUP OF FAMISHED PEOPLE

[*Face page* 104.

their bodies, which were reduced to skeletons, but they had not sufficient rags.

The children were as naked as when they were born. Their spinal cord showed a degree of curvature. Their ribs and the joints of their hands and legs were easy to number. Their heads, and at times their inflated abdomens, looked out of proportion to their emaciated bodies. On their scurfy heads grew tufts of hair. Some of the hair stuck to the sides of their heads, and some waved in the air. The part of the face immediately below the nose was unclean with a dry and white substance that came from the nostril. It seemed as if their bodies had never been washed. So much dirt had accumulated on them that it produced a feeling of repulsion in the minds of the spectators.

The hair of the women was shaggy, without oil, and unkempt. The sight was a heart-rending one. After giving an order to distribute some food and clothes to these poor sufferers and to those who were probably in the barracks, I took my seat in the train and started off.

Impression left on me.

27. My visit was too short; still, I shall never forget the impression it made on me. God forbid that such miserable scenes and sufferings should ever be witnessed again! It is wonderful how the people put up with these hardships. They had resigned every hope of a happy existence, and seemed to think man could do nothing when God himself proved unkind.

28. Before I left Baroda, I had settled every

Further sanction to meet future contingencies.

little detail of the famine administration, and had made provision for almost all future contingencies that could be reasonably foreseen. Cholera, in epidemic proportions, had already broken out on some of the works, and fears were entertained that the disease might attack all the large works as the hot season advanced. It was deemed safer to close these large works and to provide employment for the labourers nearer their own homes, in small groups. In order to meet this exigency, a further amount of one hundred thousand rupees was sanctioned by me on the eve of my departure for Europe.

NAVSARI DIVISION

LABOURERS AT WORK

[*Face page* 109.

IV.—NAVSARI DIVISION

1. Soon after the Holi holidays, I thought of visiting the Navsari division. On the 24th March I left for Songadh, ostensibly for the purpose of tiger-shooting, but really impelled by a desire to see for myself the condition of the famine-stricken inhabitants of that district.

Navsari tour. March 24th—April 1st, 1900.

Of all the divisions of the State, Navsari was the least affected; but as the famine grew with the advent of the hot season, its horrors had extended in some measure to my Navsari subjects, more especially to those forest tribes who reside in the Tapti valley. Reports reached me in several different ways that these forest tribes were not in a satisfactory condition, and were just as much in need of liberal treatment as the other three divisions.

2. Some days before I set out for Songadh, I had called the Navsari Executive Engineer to Baroda, and had, in consultation with him, settled the programme of relief-works for the people of Navsari, as well as for such other people as had been or might be sent there from other divisions in order to get relief. Because the necessities of this division were not as immediately pressing as elsewhere, it had not as yet received sufficient attention from Government, so that it was not

Programme of relief-works in Navsari.

yet provided with useful works calculated to secure a rapid development of its capabilities. Some remunerative works, however, deserved to be included in the Navsari programme, and old reports and state papers were ransacked for the purpose of tracing such irrigational schemes as had been prepared in past years. The Jhakhari river and the Bandharpara irrigational works had been regarded as hopeful projects, and the Executive Engineer was asked to draw up the schemes with all data for calculations, and to submit them for the professional opinions of experts. But these schemes were not sufficiently matured to be undertaken at once, nor were the works of so large a scale or so located as satisfactorily to serve the purposes of famine-relief. So I directed the railway-line between Kosamba and Vakal in the Velachha district, covering a length of about thirty miles, to be undertaken at once. I had not by me the materials to enable me to judge of the paying capacities of lines that I ordered to be undertaken, but I turned my general knowledge of the state of the country to use, because I was very anxious to have plenty of large relief-works on which a great number of people could be easily employed for some considerable time.

Indeed, as the famine was on the increase, I preferred to err by undertaking large doubtful works, which would certainly afford wide relief, rather than to start numerous small works, which might have the effect of ultimately leaving us without an adequate field of labour. My policy, in short, was to be content with works of a petty description in the cold weather, when the number of those needing assistance would be smaller and the general tone of health steadier.

With the advent of summer large works might safely be started, because they would certainly last till the rains had properly set in. After the burst of the monsoon, the people might once again take up small works near home. I was aware that for domestic reasons I should, sooner or later, have to go to Europe, a step I had delayed taking in January, but should perforce have to take in May ; so before leaving the country I had to sketch out the above plan of campaign, whose execution would take place in my absence.

Besides these useful and remunerative works, the programme was also made to include a large number of forest roads by the construction of which, it was believed, the forest tracts would be opened up, and their produce made more accessible by land and river. Traffic in forest products is capable of being largely augmented if facilities of transport are secured by means of better roads and speedier means of communication. These forest tracks, whose location in some cases I settled on the spot, were chiefly undertaken to provide the forest tribes with work, as they are averse to going far from their homes in quest of employment.

In addition to the irrigation projects and forest roads, there were other useful items in the programme which it is not necessary to particularise here. Nor is it essential to mention their estimated cost, the number of people they were calculated to maintain, and the length of time during which they were likely to keep labourers in employment.

Great discretion was left to the local officers in the matter of determining the order in which, and the time when, these projects were to be taken in hand. But I first explained to them the general principles that should determine the order of precedence to be given to the several works, and I added some hints about the approximate dates on which they should be started, and also pointed out the different parts of the country which the schemes were simultaneously to affect. I find that it is not a bad plan to empower local officers on the spot to start works at their own discretion, without waiting to receive the mere formal sanction of their superiors.

Where there is extreme love of form and red-tapeism, it is useful sometimes to break through set forms and vest the subordinate officers with a considerable amount of discretion.

General aspect of the country.

3. On my way to Songadh I observed from my train what was the condition of the soil I traversed, how the country looked in general, in what state was the physical condition of the people and cattle,—and so gradually formed my own views on the subject. The trees on the roadside were not quite leafless as in parts of Baroda; the cattle were not emaciated; grass and hay stacks were seen at intervals at different railway stations and villages, and the general appearance of the country was not quite as desolate as in the other parts of my dominions.

Meeting with the officers.

4. As soon as I reached the Songadh station, I noticed that the road to the town, the making of which I had suggested at the time of my previous visit, had not been undertaken. The water-works scheme for the town of Songadh

also had not yet passed the stage of discussion and correspondence. I ordered the former to be included in the programme of works immediately to be taken in hand, and desired the Chief Engineer to expedite the determination about the latter. I asked the Subha, who was with me in my carriage, how the famine measures were progressing in his district. He was new to the division, and did not seem to know as much of the progress on the works and of the needs of his district as he ought to have done. He answered some of my questions, but before doing so fully on all points, and furnishing me with authentic statistics, he begged to be allowed to look up his notes and to discuss matters with the local Naib Subha, Mr. Vaidya.

As soon as I reached the new Mahal Kacheri, I sent for the Subha, the Naib Subha, the Executive Engineer, the Conservator of Forests, the Vahivatdar, and some representative people of the town, and asked them to give me their suggestions and any information that was likely to be of use to me.

I discussed certain points in connection with the problem of famine-relief with the local officers. I was surprised to learn that the Subha had not in his hands the famine programme which had been sanctioned for his division. The Executive Engineer and my Secretary were asked to furnish him with a copy. The Subha, the Executive Engineer, and the Conservator of Forests were requested, after mutual consultation, to fix the time when, and the order in which, the relief-works should be started according to the varying necessities of the different districts, and to give me a copy of their joint recommendation. I impressed upon them the necessity of working energetically and in unison, and begged each to keep an open mind in the discussion of any question, and not to allow himself to be moved by any prejudice or partiality for any department.

Grass operation.

5. I also used the opportunity of my stay at Songadh to find out what was the general impression as to the manner in which the grass affair had been managed by the local officers. I had heard a good deal about this matter while in Baroda, and had ordered several steps to be taken which should have tended to evolve order out of chaos. It is most vexatious to see how matters are allowed to drift before a conclusion is arrived at and action taken.

The initial outlay required for the purchase of grass had been drawn by the Khetivadi Kamdar from the balance of the agricultural bank at Songadh; and as the money realised from the proceeds of the sale of the grass had not yet been returned to the bank, the Vahivatdar represented to me the financial difficulties and straits to which that institution had been reduced. Orders were passed by me to recoup the balance from the State Treasury till the money withdrawn from the bank was returned by the Khetivadi Kamdar.

Poorhouse for Songadh.

6. I stopped only a few hours at Songadh. On my way to Amkooti I saw the poorhouse for the Songadh Taluka, and made some inquiries about the condition of its inmates. I found that the institution was maintained by private charity, and that the inmates were not given

a sufficient quantity of food. The general sanction accorded by the Government to the opening of poorhouses had not yet been received by the local officers. The grass-cutting operations, in which large numbers of people had been employed, were over, and the time for the Government to open a few of these poorhouses for the whole division had arrived. I accordingly sanctioned 10,000 rupees for the expenses of the poorhouse, and directed that my general order about gratuitous relief should be made applicable to those parts of the Navsari division where the effects of the famine had assumed a definite form.

Petitions for remission of assessment.

7. On the way to Amkooti petitions were presented me at several places by the people of these Kali praj (forest) tribes asking for remission on the ground of—the stock argument—the famine. This behaviour was not quite new to me, as I had seen it before in my previous trips. These poor and guileless people are put up by their creditors, Parsi liquor-sellers and Government servants, to beg for remission. I was reminded of the great necessity for finishing the survey and settlement of these Talukas, and wrote a letter directing the department to carry out the operation as soon as circumstances would permit of it. The present system of land revenue in this Taluka places these poor people too much at the mercy of local officials. I am thinking of trying in these districts the "varying Bighoti" system, which is expected to combine the advantages of both the Bighoti and the Bhagbatai systems. I never realised how crushing were the effects of the Bighoti or fixed cash

assessment system till the present year of famine, and never did I receive more petitions and requests for saving the people from the burden of the Bighoti, whose incidence is every year the same, irrespective of the prospects of the season. Had circumstances permitted, nothing would have given me greater pleasure than to suspend or even to remit the land revenues for this year of exceptional calamity ; but, alas ! the resources of a Native State are not boundless. Under the old system the Government probably took more in good times; but it also showed great generosity in the grant of remissions during hard times like these.

Forest tribes of Songadh.

8. During my stay at Amkooti I visited the houses of some of these Kali praj (forest) people and talked with them, and I may be excused for leaving the main subject of this little work of mine to say something regarding a class of people whom I have always regarded with peculiar interest. I have another reason for allowing this somewhat lengthy digression to remain among the recorded notes of my itinerary. It shows how, while I was in Songadh, I was at liberty to divert my attention for a time from the usually all-absorbing anxiety regarding the famine. This proves that here, at any rate, matters were not so serious as elsewhere, and that I could afford to give my mind a holiday, a pleasant and healthy rebound from a persistent state of tension.

I was glad to find that these people were less timid at the approach of strangers than were some cognate tribes whom I had seen.

Dress.

It was very interesting to observe their

manners and customs, their mode of living, their dress and their appearance. The males among these tribes rarely wear turbans. On the other hand, they are dressed in short jackets and scarves (dhotars), which last, when worn, somewhat resemble in appearance the Italian military overcoat. At home they put on nothing but a small piece of cloth (langoti) tied round the loins and a small tape wound about the head. Ordinarily the women wear no bodices, and exhibit with a kind of pride, and certainly without any shyness, a bounteous development of bosom; but of late some of them have taken to the more refined fashion of covering their breasts. They have only a thick piece of coloured scarf (chehayal) which goes round the loins and passes up behind the back, exhibiting firm well-rounded limbs some inches above the knees. One end of their coloured raiment is tied up on the head, either to give them greater facility while carrying a burden, or to prevent the hair from being dishevelled.

Ornaments.

They freely indulge in their barbaric love of personal ornaments by wearing clusters of beads and heaps of coloured shells round their necks. They put on a number of anklets, made of brass, which make a peculiar tinkling sound when they move. The beads and shells are mostly imported from Europe and countries far from the shores of India. Their boys and girls wear practically nothing, except sometimes a little rag wrapped round the hips.

Marriage.

Wedding expenses amongst them are not heavy, a marriage usually not costing more than fifty rupees. Marital ties are loose and can be easily broken; though the women are generally said to be chaste while living with the men they have taken for their husbands. Matrimonial contracts are entered into as the result of mutual choice, and are dissolved at pleasure.

Aversion to Banias, etc.

They have a natural dread of the Bania, who, as they think, loots them, and their aversion to the money-lender is often manifested in a striking form.

General characteristics.

They have no love for Government officials, especially for the police, and they are nervously afraid of their periodical visits. The Maharaja's visits, I am told, form an exception to this, because his advent gives them labour, which brings in wages, and, still more, because he protects them from harassment and gives them banquets and drinking bouts, besides clothes to wear. They have strong caste feelings and prejudices, and do not consider themselves a bit inferior to their fellow-mortals. Their religion consists chiefly in the worship of stone images, and they have a staunch belief in the efficacy of witchcraft and the dangers of the evil eye. The Brahmin finds no place in their religious ceremonies. Their feasts generally consist of a good drink and a hearty dance, in which both sexes join on terms of perfect equality.

Character.

These people are extremely truthful, and their artlessness often sends them to the jail and the scaffold. However, the modern system of law-courts and Vakeels will soon teach them the ways of chicanery and prevarication. They are also, and naturally so, very cowardly, because all spirit, even that of rational resistance, has been completely crushed out of them by long oppression and by the unsympathetic treatment they must have received from unfriendly tribes and races, who had driven them to take shelter in these sterile and malarious lands, in the vicinity of ferocious wild beasts, and far away from the influences of settled society. Such were the people for whom I had to devise relief-measures : contented, because ignorant ; quiet, because powerless to resist ; living in scattered hamlets, owing to their not knowing that union is strength ; virtuous, because they had no temptations to overcome.

More might be mentioned here of their household utensils, the size and nature of their rooms, and the materials of which their houses are constructed ; the way they store up their stock of grain for the year ; their cattle-sheds ; how ingeniously they utilise the bamboo in the construction of ladders ; their language ; their domestic pet animals ; their mode of treating guests ; the objections they have against settling down in any one fixed locality,—but details of this kind would demand a larger space than I care to afford.

Their condition during the famine period.

9. We met with several tribes or clans of these Kali praj (forest) tribes in the neighbourhood of Songadh. There are (1) Dubalas, (2) Dhankas, (3) Chondharas, (4) Naikdas, (5) Bhils, and (6) Konkanees, who speak a dialect which is a mixture of a low form of Marathi and Gujarathi. The material condition of these people, even in ordinary times, is so wretched as to excite compassion. They live exclusively on roots and herbs and leaves and flowers during certain parts of the year. In the course of my tour

I noticed a few of these people who were really out of condition; but as a class I did not find that they were so badly off as they would have been had they lived in the other famine-stricken parts of the Raj. Notwithstanding this impression, I sanctioned a large number of relief-works for them in the Navsari programme.

The evils of delay before the necessary sanctions could be obtained from a centralised government had been repeatedly brought to my notice during my tours; and, trusting to the idea that in a one-man-rule form of government decentralisation is most conducive to despatch of business, I gave the local officers discretionary powers to start any work out of the famine programme for the division estimated to cost not more than 6000 rupees.

Forest produce.

10. At Amkooti I realised the splendid use which might be made of the forest products towards the industrial development of the country. Chips of bamboos cut in these forests could have been very usefully employed in the construction of mats and thatched roofs for sheds on many of our relief-works. I sanctioned 6000 rupees for the purpose, and directed the Conservator of Forests to employ local labour on the work of supplying materials for sheds on the different centres of relief. The idea had, however, to be given up as impracticable.

Land improvement scheme.

11. The local officers were also directed to start some relief-works at once for the benefit of the Songadh people, and to see me at Amkooti after making all the necessary arrangements for setting them on foot. The Naib Subha came to my camp and submitted several relief-schemes for my sanction. He represented that there was

great scope for the improvement of the land in the district; and if advances of money were tendered to the cultivators on easy terms, he was of opinion that they would diligently attempt to improve the productive powers of the soil by damming up water in kyaris (little squares). At his request I sanctioned 30,000 rupees for the Vyara and Mahuva districts, and empowered him and the Vahivatdar to make loans to the cultivators on terms similar to those I had sanctioned for the tagavi for new wells in the Kadi and Baroda divisions. The Subha then requested an extension of the same boon to other parts of his Division, and 30,000 rupees were sanctioned for such tagavi advances for the whole Navsari district. This amount, coupled with the 25,000 rupees previously sanctioned out of the general grant for new wells for the whole Raj, was deemed quite sufficient to meet all demands for tagavi for the purposes of land improvement.

Tagavi for maintenance and for grass.

12. It was also brought to my notice that there was a large number of poor but respectable men in the district who were prevented from resorting to the relief-works by social sentiment and family pride. To relieve them from the pangs of starvation, I sanctioned a sum of 15,000 rupees for tagavi advances for the purpose of maintenance. Another sum of 15,000 rupees was also sanctioned for tagavi for grass. Though there was plenty of grass in the district, many of the impoverished cultivators had not the means to purchase any for the support of their cattle. They were willing to receive State help in the form of such tagavi, and orders were issued that they should be supplied with grass.

Mr. Vaidya, the Naib Subha.

13. Many of these suggestions proceeded from Mr. Vaidya, the Naib Subha of the division, with whom I was glad to have come into contact. He is an intelligent and energetic officer, of an inquiring turn of mind, though circumspect in action. He seemed to take great interest in the welfare of the State, and to have some of the good qualities of the officers of the older generation. His knowledge of English is not of a very high order, nor are his educational qualifications of a distinguished kind ; but his mind and body are more active and practieal than is generally the case with the feebler and less practical products of our present system of instruction.

Education promoted among the forest tribes.

14. I spent a pleasant week at Amkooti, and greatly enjoyed my stay on the banks of the Tapti in the midst of the simple forest people. I often inquired of them why they did not send their children to Songadh, and whether I could take some of them and their children with me to Baroda, a request they all refused. They said they were quite happy where they were. Some of the more advanced amongst them expressed their willingness to send their children to Songadh, where they knew that they would be educated and brought up entirely at Government expense. I directed my officers to send some orphans from the district to the Songadh Boarding School. I was very glad to notice that the people seemed more inclined to educate their children than before. I directed that some of the usual village dues that were not required for these Rani Mahals (forest tracts) should be diverted to the Educational Department and

CHILDREN FITTED FOR WORK IN THE VISNAGAR ANNAGRUHA [Face page 122.

expended in prizes for both teachers and pupils, and in scholarships for the latter, to induce them to attend the primary schools in large numbers. It is my firm conviction that for the good of our country every class of our people, without any distinction of caste, creed, or profession, should be well educated. I consider good education to be absolutely necessary, not only to awaken our sleeping countrymen to a sense of their abject and servile condition, but also to enable them to produce the best and the largest number of commodities possible at the least cost of labour, and to fit them to study successfully the conditions of markets at home and abroad. Without it, the present social and national deterioration cannot be stayed, the present political and industrial decline cannot be arrested. These forest tribes are human beings of undeveloped reason, and education alone can evolve the latent faculty in them. I noticed a great number of their boys under twelve loitering about in the villages doing practically nothing to help their parents. I thought of the waste of power, the economic loss entailed on family and country, which was the result of our neglect in training these children. The experiment of educating them in boarding schools is being tried in the division, and I leave it to the future to judge of its results.

15. After spending some days in shikar in the Vajpur forest, I went away for a short time to see my people at Lanavali: thence I returned to Baroda to give my final sanction to the prospective arrangements of the famine administration before leaving for Europe. In order to enable me to get an approximate idea of the probable Conclusion.

cost we might have to incur in the future, and also to spare my officers the necessity of adopting the tardy and circuitous system of asking for my sanction on each separate occasion, I ordered the Subhas and other officers, through my Minister, to prepare the famine programme and to submit for sanction all the prospective requirements of the Famine Administration. I was anxious to see that, as the famine grew worse, the munificence of the Government should become more and more marked; and with this object in view, where my officers solicited sanction for forty lacs, I accorded my sanction to fifty lacs as the maximum future expenditure.

Famine policy expounded.

16. Having settled the famine programme and provided for all future requirements, I proceeded to Sankheda to lay the foundation-stone of the large irrigation work at Jhojwa on the Orsang river. On this occasion I made a speech which contains, in the rough, some of my views on the famine policy.

The Chief Engineer's report, which was read on the occasion, contained the following brief account of the project:—

"Your Highness, Ladies and Gentlemen,—We have come here this morning to witness the inauguration of this irrigation scheme, which is now to be commenced. Before asking your Highness to lay the foundation-stone of this work, I think it will be interesting to you and the public if I give a short account of what is proposed to be done, and what the prospective advantages of this scheme are likely to be.

"This river Orsang, which is to be dammed for irrigational purposes, rises in the Dhar State, and flows through the State of Chhota-Udeypur to our boundary near Bodeli, 7 miles above here, draining an area of over 800 square miles, and it is this flow after the flood-waters pass in the monsoon that is to be utilised by this dam and head works, and carried along 30 miles of channels which will be made to irrigate the lands in the Sankheda Taluka.

"We are particularly fortunate in having this outcrop of rock at this site, as it enables the dam to be built in a comparatively easy way, and establishes the scheme as a financial success. The site, I believe, was brought to the Subha Saheb's notice by the district ex-engineer some years ago, and Mr. Khaserao so impressed his Highness with its advantages, that he ordered its thorough investigation, and it was found in every way suitable to our needs.

"The masonry dam which will be commenced to-day will be a structure about 25,000 feet long, 12 feet wide at the base, and 10 feet at the top, and be raised to a level of 6 feet above the river-bed in the centre, and 10 feet at the flanks, and is estimated to cost 2½ lacs of rupees. It will be made of sufficient width and strength that the surplus water, after the rains have stopped, may eventually be impounded, and the level of the impounding area raised either by means of weir-boards or automatic sluices. From observations that have been made, there seems to be very little doubt that in ordinary years of rainfall we shall have a good flow of water 140 feet per second up to the end of January; and by addition of some arrangement for impounding the flood-water here and at the Motipura Nulla, the quantity we shall have at our disposal will be available longer. This quantity of water, after allowing for loss by evaporation, will be sufficient for irrigating 20,000 Bighas.

"The main channel will be about 13 miles, and there will be one branch channel about 5 miles, and another 12 miles long.

"Approximately the total cost of the scheme will be 10 lakhs.

"The main channel will irrigate land in Bhulwan, Herekna, Lotia, Akhtiarpur, Gamri, Bahadarpur, Charmatuva, Bhaopura, Kalitalaori, Motipura, Simalia, and Mota-Virpura, the tail-water eventually going into the Dhadar river near the last-named village.

"The 5-mile branch will irrigate lands in Vithalpura, Balapur, Simalia, Akoti, Suwarja, Punsoli, and Dengiward, the tail-water going again to Dhadar, near that village.

"The other branch will irrigate lands in the villages of Vithalpura, Chhapra, Motipura, Wadwana, Sameherpura, Khariakuwa, Boriad, Kudad, Dameli Dabhoi, Therwasa, and Habipura, the tail-water going to the Rah near the last-mentioned village.

"When such favourable prospects for this project were explained to your Highness, you decided that the scheme was worth carrying out, and I am glad to say you have since been assured of this by a very favourable report Mr. Whiting, the irrigation expert, has made on the whole scheme.

"I now ask your Highness to kindly lay the first stone of this large work, at the same time expressing the hope that it will be speedily and satisfactorily completed after what I am convinced will be such an auspicious commencement."

The speech which I then made was to the following effect :—

"Gentlemen,—My first duty, before opening this work to-day, is a very pleasant one. It is to thank the officers to whose exertions and intelligence the institution of this work is mainly due. And first I have to thank Mr. Khaserao for his suggestion of the idea. The acuteness and intelligence which made him perceive the possibilities of the site deserve every praise. (Cheers.) I have also to thank the engineers for the zeal and energy with which they have arranged the working details of the scheme. Their professional ability has given a working shape to an excellent and highly practicable idea. Their example is worthy of imitation ; both the mental activity and shrewdness which suggested, and the professional talent and energy which worked out the scheme. I trust that the execution of the work will be as sound and thorough as its inception, and that I may again have occasion to thank them for completing ably what they have ably initiated. (Cheers.)

"The relief-work I am opening to-day is of some magnitude. Beneficial results beyond mere temporary relief are expected from it. Such an undertaking is a fit response to the sombre warning of the terrible visitation under which the country is suffering. This famine is one which falls with a lamentably heavy insistence on man, cattle, and field. It has dried up the land like some terrific and all-pervading curse. It has destroyed not only the objects of agriculture, but its living instruments. It threatens to impoverish the future while it is devastating the present. Not only so, but it is in the nature of a divine admonition. For it points with terrible emphasis to the disastrous economic condition of the people, on which all progress and government ultimately rest. It warns both Government and people that a great problem must be speedily grappled with. If from indolence or ignorance they neglect it, it will be on peril of stagnation, deterioration, and decay.

"When face to face with a calamity of this sort the first pressing need a Government feels is to relieve the stricken population in whose welfare it feels its own involved. Taking this task by itself, and excluding for a moment wider considerations, we have to notice that there are different methods of meeting the problem. The danger is that in the first pressing impulse to do something, administrations may be led to adopt a sketchy and undigested programme, such a programme as fits more or less adequately the immediate want, but has no eye to the future. This they are especially likely to do if they are unprepared for a great calamity.

"Two things only can help us to avoid mistakes of this sort: experience well used, or an intellectual and scientific spirit of administration. To us, experience of famine—that bitter teacher—has been wanting, at least on any large scale. For never before within the memory of more than one generation has the scourge fallen so heavily on this fertile province. And this is a deficiency on which we may congratulate ourselves.

"But an administration so situated should be all the more careful to study the experience of less-favoured regions. It should forecast wisely, though not dogmatically, the probable extent of the evil. It should suit its programme thereto, though always ready to modify or develop as circumstances demand. It should weigh carefully the different methods of relief open to it, and use all skilfully and prudently, and should encourage those chiefly which are most pregnant of future benefit.

"The officers of the administration should avoid on the one hand all cast-iron routine, the tendency to resort to which is growing to a disheartening extent. On the other hand, the other extreme of scratch-work should be equally avoided. They should ascertain and master the general lines of policy to be followed. They should guide themselves along these and yet keep testing their value by practical facts, and they should always be ready to offer fruitful and well-considered suggestions. Mistakes in details, unsuccessful tentatives, will probably be inevitable at first. But a firm grasp of principles, joined to a keen eye and an open mind, will surely remove all defects. These qualities, aided by fuller experience, will ensure, we may fairly hope, as harmonious and perfect a system as is humanly possible.

"Relief measures may, roughly speaking, be divided into three classes according to their final results. The first consists of such measures as give relief merely and go no further. It is necessary to avail oneself of these to a limited extent, especially where they take the shape of poorhouses, doles, or advances, etc. Such measures are needed to save the lives of those who can do no work, whether from excessive suffering and emaciation, or from social position. The latter is the case of purdah women and others, whose status or habits prevent them from seeking relief even when perishing from hunger. For, even if we disregard humane feelings altogether, the lives of citizens, especially those of the workers, are the valuable assets of a community. But I need hardly say that where there is no imperative need for, and no special advantage is to be gained by, this sort of relief, measures more obviously productive should be preferred.

"Measures of the second class are those which are productive in an indirect way, such as opening new means of communication. The most important of these are, of course, railways. Much doubt has been felt as to the advantage of a network of railways, and more especially if, from the point of view of a famine, it is an unmixed blessing. It is certain that the rail carries out the surplus produce which formerly there was a reasonable chance of storing in the country itself. It may be argued on the other side that it facilitates import as well as export. Weighing the question carefully, it may be fair to conclude that the area of a famine, when it occurs, is extended by the existence of railways, though very possibly its local effects are mitigated.

"But the advantages of a railway system to

trade and commerce, especially if its construction is unfettered by artificial restrictions, are incalculable. It may, therefore, fairly be regarded as a means of famine-relief, advantageous to the future prosperity of the country. Naturally, however, a full use of the rail cannot be realised until the country wakes from its lethargy and throws some energy into the creation of new industries.

"Measures of the third class are those which are directly productive, and are, therefore, not only a relief to present, but a prevention of future, famines. Means of communication help to circulate production, but cease for the time to be advantageous when there is no production to circulate. Irrigation works, on the other hand, the sinking of wells, the making of dams, the cutting of irrigation canals, directly increase production, and guard, so far as they go, against famine.

"These, therefore, are the most suitable measures of all for famine-relief work. Giving tagavi for well-sinking is one of the most satisfactory of such measures, because it unites Government assistance with self-help in the cultivator. But there are other devices which are more momentous, because larger in conception and more widespread in their effects. To them the work which I am opening to-day belongs, and I place on the same level the great reservoir at Kadarpur in the Kadi division, and other large works of a similar kind which have been started or are in contemplation.

"In parts of the State where irrigation on a great scale is not possible, but where it is practicable to sink wells, it is intended that the latter should be turned out in profusion, and for this purpose two lakhs annually have been set apart by the State, of which I hope the people will take advantage.

"The State has grudged no means of relief to the afflicted population, but has used all, I hope and believe, in their right places. It has liberally provided poorhouses in all affected districts. It has made ungrudging advances to those who are temporarily distressed but are precluded by their social position or other valid causes from resorting to the relief-works. It has attempted in several ways to restrict the mortality of the cattle. It has started such works as road-making and repairs, tanks, etc., to meet immediate needs. It has commenced to lay the earthwork of new railways, which, though it forms but a fraction of the cost of constructing railways, is all that can at present be done in the country. It has freely given tagavi to cultivators for well-sinking and other purposes. To-day it is opening a work which will be of permanent agricultural benefit to whole districts.

"In its methods it has been actuated by an earnest desire to use the best. It has been actuated by a spirit of the most humane and open-minded consideration for the people, united with principles of good administration. And if any errors of detail have been committed, they have been, or are being, corrected.

"Relief measures on a large scale impress the imagination and deservedly excite the encomiums of the people for their noble humanity. But those in authority should not be blinded by these praises. They should remember that these encomiums will be short-lived unless the measures which are undertaken go deep, that is, prove of lasting benefit through the wisdom of their design.

"So much for the means of meeting the immediate calamity. But we shall surely be blind and imbecile if we stop here, and neglect the broader lessons which this terrible experience of famine ought to impel us to learn. For relief measures merely palliate the evil, but do not for a moment strike at its root. And if it is allowed to grow, eventually the resources even of the richest Government will be baffled by it.

"How is it that the people of this country have fallen into such a condition that stamina seems altogether wanting in them? The failure of rain for a single season has come with crushing force upon them. It has left them naked of resources, it has thrown ever more and more thousands and hundreds of thousands on the charity of Government relief! What are the reasons of this disastrous condition of things and by what remedies can it be met? This is what should engage the earnest attention of those in authority.

"Now, though I cannot indicate here all the minor causes and issues, yet the grand total in which they are summed up is indisputable; it is the great poverty of the people. Improved communications have provided sufficient means of supply from outside when the harvest within the country fails. But of what use are these if there is no money to purchase such supplies? Poverty is the great fact in India. And to this, I fear, I must add many defects of character, of which perhaps poverty is partly a result and partly a parent source: want of real thrift, want of energy and enterprise, of legitimate ambition and a high ideal; passiveness, fatalism, and supineness in the face of calamity. Unless this state of things is removed, unless the people can be taught self-help, it seems inevitable that things should go from bad to worse.

"I have often mixed with people and talked with them. I have conversed with the people individually and collectively, known and unknown, at my place and on the scenes of works, by day and by night. Moreover, lest my position should exclude me from correct impressions, I have also ascertained the feelings of the multitude through officials and non-officials, men of all grades. And I have been struck by the helplessness and passiveness of the people. Their spirits seem to be so cramped, dull, and inelastic. The notion that they might make energetic use of their faculties, especially in the presence of adversity, seems to be so foreign to their mental habits.

"But behind this poverty, connected with this absence of self-help, is another great characteristic fact. The population of India depends almost entirely on two means of subsistence: the educated classes look to Government service, the uneducated dare not go beyond agriculture. On the causes of this we need not at present touch, but the fact is there.

"Now, it is indisputable that countries like Russia and India, which have large populations, yet depend almost entirely on agriculture, can never be safe against famine. The secret of

European prosperity is the prevalence of manufacturing industries. If we look at England, we find whole counties like Lancashire and the Midlands wholly given up to industries. We find great cities devoted mainly to some particular manufacture; as Manchester to cotton, Sheffield to cutlery, Glasgow to shipbuilding, Birmingham to arms, machinery, and other ironwork. And it is these counties and cities which are the basis of England's prosperity. With their wealth she is able to buy her food from abroad and disregard rain and drought, good season and bad season.

"It is not possible, if it were desirable, for India to become such a predominatingly manufacturing country as England is. But to lessen the degree in which the one pursuit of agriculture absorbs all our energies is absolutely necessary for our self-preservation. The example of Germany and Japan, which have been so successfully raising themselves from poor countries to the rank of great manufacturing countries, ought to be a spur and an encouragement to us.

"It will be for us, as far as in us lies, to take the lesson of the famine to heart and set ourselves to encourage the growth of trades and industries. It may be done in various ways. We may give all reasonable facilities to many kinds of enterprise; we may provide for and encourage education in different directions. Finally, where possible and advisable, initial measures of protection and bounty may be adopted. It would surely not be unwise if infant industries, which have to struggle against fully developed and powerful competition, were to receive some protection in the beginning. This need only be continued until they have reached a stage where they may be accounted safe from being smothered in their birth. The theory and practice of all undeveloped countries may safely be followed to this limited extent in India, which the competition of machinery has thrown back into the rank of undeveloped countries. Lastly, I would encourage and promote emigration, either within or without the country.

"But, whatever encouragement and help the Government may give, it can do nothing unless there is self-help on the part of the people. Education, by instruction and example, is the great begetter of self-help. But it is the misfortune of India that its educated sons choose to be as helpless and unenterprising as the ignorant. For they allow their horizon to be limited by the alluring prospects of Government service. The educated class must break through the bonds of apathy and dependence. They must begin to work out new careers for themselves in a spirit of manliness and self-reliance. Then only can any sensible improvement take place. When educated enterprise and self-help, backed by the assistance and encouragement of States and Governments, unite, then will begin an era which will speedily make such lamentable experiences as the present year's a thing antiquated and impossible. (Loud cheers.)"

Before I conclude, I must reiterate what I have often said, that the salvation of the people lies in their own hands. Easily impressionable, easily pleased, credulous, devoid of any knowledge of their own claims, our race possesses a very short memory, and is practically without any record of history.

This is not well. The first and most necessary step is that our people should keep in mind the causes of their misfortunes, and examine whether the ills they suffer from are the natural result of their own shortcomings or institutions, or are of artificial creation by others. This ascertained, they must next earnestly and resolutely endeavour to remedy these evils. God helps those who help themselves. He does not help those who look to external assistance for all good things, or are dismayed by hope deferred, failures and disappointments. For it is as true now as it ever was, that the law of this world requires struggle and self-sacrifice as the purchase-money of success, and will extort every penny of the price before it gives an adequate return.

The institution of Government is indeed inevitable, but it is not so efficient, economical, and powerful as private bodies often are in the management of their own affairs. Government gets its money by taxing either all or a part of its subjects, and in return spends a portion of it in helping the thoughtless, and those reduced to want through no fault of their own, through periods of exceptional distress.

Our people would find it more economical and more gratifyng to self-respect if they learned to husband their own resources, and to do away as much as possible with the costly intervention of Government. They would probably have to pay less, and would certainly have to suffer less from the effects of demoralisation.

Last year, though the rains did not set in in time, the people hoped against hope till about November, expecting the fall of rain—a piece of conduct entirely consistent with their credulous confidence in fate, and in breaches of natural law. They will have to learn to water their own crops as soon as the rains hold off. I am supplying a large number of wells and means of irrigation which should be turned to good account. These new means of mitigating the severity of famine have certain attendant evils. But with prudence and foresight on the part of the cultivators, these can be minimised. Good manuring, drainage, and abstention from over-working the fields for immediate profit are of the utmost and most essential importance.

Conclusion. The object of these pages has been merely to give my personal impressions of the famine, and of the measures taken to relieve it. I have purposely avoided giving any information which is likely to be contained in the official Famine Report, which I expect to get in course of time. In that report I hope to have the work of every officer and department mentioned and properly delineated. I have touched upon such points only of a general Report as I could not avoid without leaving my narrative incomplete. There is one fact which I cannot help mentioning, as its omission would fail to give a complete picture of my impressions. It is that, notwithstanding the multifarious duties imposed on them by sundry departments and innumerable superiors, the strain caused by bad times has been cheerfully borne by the servants of the State belonging to all departments and to all grades and ranks of the service. From the highest, the Minister, to the lowest, all with great unanimity and earnestness have done their honest best to help the poor and the afflicted. At no time have I found the spirit of philanthropy so actively exhibited as during the unprecedentedly bad times we have gone through. From the people I have often heard sober and sensible words, the sincerity of which could not fail to impress one. They expressed the feeling that Government had done a great deal for the community in these trying times.

I know there are critics of native administration, some in power and some not, who are only too ready to note what are the obligations of Native States, and too slow to consider what are their means of discharging them—critics who are apt to apply to the States and their mode of administration tests which savour of a want of genuine sympathy and a lack of real acquaintance with their circumstances. Notwithstanding such adverse criticism, and in spite of certain defects in the execution of the famine measures, some of which have already been noticed in these pages, I may say with all modesty that the State has, after gauging the requirements of the season, and after taking into consideration the present and future welfare of its subjects, done its best to lighten the sufferings of the people.

I take this opportunity of heartily thanking my various officers for their wise suggestions and counsels. I have not attempted to do so in these pages. Without the help and sympathy of his subordinate fellow-workers, a person in authority might just as well think to make bricks without straw as to achieve any considerable success. I may here remark, *en passant*, that I have come across a few officers who had sufficient stuff in them to leave their impress on the pages of history had they been granted more scope, and were not the times unfavourable to the development of their genius. In order that my readers may be in a position to appreciate the good work of my official and non-official co-operators in the good work of relief, a list of names, yet incomplete, has been appended.

Knowing that everything had been clearly thought out which could possibly be foreseen, having also full confidence in the sagacity and fidelity of the Minister and his colleagues, I entrusted the execution and the finish of the famine administration to their care, and to them do I ungrudgingly give full credit for the execution of my policy.

APPENDIX

I.—Prominent Mention of those who took a conspicuous part in the Famine Work

The names of persons who took a prominent part in the famine work of the last year are given below, in connection with matters in which they rendered useful services.

TOURS

Tours of His Highness the Maharaja.—In connection with famine measures, the most notable event is that of the tours of His Highness the Maharaja Saheb, in all divisions, with a view personally to see the state of things, and to adopt remedial measures on the spot. The utility and importance of such tours cannot be overrated. A great many of the measures, referred to under their proper heads, which would have taken much time to reach the Huzur, through so many officers, were discussed with the local officials and the people, and sanctioned on the spot. The initiative also of many of the orders, that were afterwards issued from Baroda, can be traced to the inquiries made during the tours. His Highness's visit to any one division was productive of much good not only to the people of that division, but, in many cases, to all, by the application to other divisions of orders of general usefulness. Many of the orders and sanctions about water-supply, fodder-supply, and tagavi, applicable to all divisions, were issued during or after his visit to the Kadi division in the month of December. In addition to these, special measures, such as the opening of an orphanage at Mehsana, hospitals for sick women, the free gift of food to the needy in Harij and other places, were the results of this visit; and most of them had made a start by the end of December. In the months of January and February His Highness paid a visit to the Amreli division, when other orders were passed for the good of the people. Prominent among these were the sanctions of the programme of relief-works, on an extensive scale, for the Amreli division, and of large amounts for sinking wells, for drinking and agricultural purposes, in the Kodinar, Dhari, and Damnagar Mahals. Orders were also given for the improvement of Velan Bandar, for the employment of additional hands in the Public Works, Revenue, and Police Departments, and for advancing tagavi to Kheduts for the purchase of seeds and for maintenance. The opening of kitchens for children was ordered on some works. Seeing that the Vahivatdars and Mahalkaris were overburdened with the additional famine work, His Highness was pleased to relieve them of their magisterial work, entrusting it to special magistrates or Munsiffs. In the Baroda division His Highness's inquiry was continuous. . . . At Dabka, on receiving applications from the people, in October, he granted immediate sanctions for tagavi, and referred the other points for report to the Revenue officers. When His Highness visited the Petlad-Cambay Railway and Karamsad drainage-works, he found that the piece-work system that was adopted there told greatly against the weak and emaciated labourers, and he was pleased to order that a separate small work or a section of the big work should always be assigned to such labourers, and that they should be paid under the task-work rules. Finding again that the rates paid on these works were inadequate for the maintenance of labourers, he was pleased to increase them at once. Kitchens were ordered to be opened for children under seven years. The cold season being devoted to tours in the Kadi and

Amreli divisions, His Highness visited in March the most affected parts of the Rani Mahals of the Navsari division. . . . Large sanctions for gratuitous relief in the Navsari division, for tagavi to Kheduts for the purchase of grass and seed, and for maintenance, as well as for sinking wells in the Vyara and Mahuva Mahals, already noted in their proper places, were granted, while His Highness was moving in the Songadh Rani Mahal. The Subha and the Executive Engineer of the division were empowered to sanction conjointly and to start at once urgent relief-works, so that no delay might occur in granting timely relief. Sanctions for the employment of additional establishments in the Kadi and Baroda divisions for village inspection and for the supervision of works in the Amreli division were granted ; and several orders relating to all divisions were passed at the same time. On inspecting the Songadh poorhouse, His Highness found that a sufficient quantity of food was not given to the inmates according to the code ; and he was pleased to enforce at once the provisions of the code, asking for an explanation from those through whose oversight the mistake was committed. From this hasty review of His Highness's tours, it will be perceived that many remedial measures were adopted on the spot, which, otherwise, would have remained unnoticed or would have taken many days before they reached the Huzur. . . .

His Excellency the Dewan Saheb's Tour.—His Excellency the Dewan Saheb, who had from the outset completely identified himself with the direction of all famine operations, visited many places in order personally to see the condition of the people and the adequacy of the measures adopted for their relief. Though his heavy work in the capital city did not allow him to be away from it repeatedly or for any length of time, His Excellency, during the year under report, visited eight out of the ten Mahals of Kadi. His inquiries were minute ; and he collected much valuable information, and saw the leading relief-works and poorhouses.

This, of course, resulted in many useful instructions and orders.

Tours of the Huzur Officers.—The following table shows, in brief, the details of the tours of the Huzur famine officers :—

NAME OF THE OFFICER.	Days travelled.	Villages inspected.	Poorhouses inspected.	Relief-works inspected.
1	2	3	4	5
Meherban Rao Bahadur Ramchandra Vithoba Dhamnaskar, Sar Subha	113	41	10	23
Mr. Jamshedjee Ardeshir Dalal, Famine Commissioner	99	38	11	21
Mr. Ramchandra Abaji Raje, Assistant to the Famine Commissioner	37	45	8	16
Mr. Manchharam Bhagvanji, 2nd Assistant to the Famine Commissioner	10	1	3	1
Total	259	125	32	61

From the above it will be seen that the Huzur famine officers travelled 259 days; and during this period they inspected 125 villages, 32 poorhouses, and 61 relief-works in the year under report. From the full diaries and reports of these officers, it will be seen that their inspections were careful and useful. In inspecting relief-works and poorhouses they had to make searching inquiries on no less than 98 special points, to which their attention was directed by standing orders. They also obtained orders or suggestions from higher authorities on matters beyond their powers.

The heads of the Medical and Police Departments also were constantly in the districts, in order effectively to supervise the famine work of their subordinates and establishments. The Chief Engineer, who had to devote the greater portion of his time to the famine work, travelled 126 days on famine duty, and inspected 56 works during the year under report. Some of the important works he visited more than once.

II.—Poorhouses and other Charities

Indian Famine Charitable Relief Fund.—His Highness's Government can never be sufficiently thankful to Colonel Ravenshaw, the Resident, through whose advocacy Baroda was enabled to secure a large sum from the Indian Charitable Relief Fund, out of which Rs. 2,15,000 were disbursed before the end of July last. This afforded very valuable help both in relieving the destitute and in enabling the resourceless to resume their usual occupations.

Donors in Kadi Division.—The names of the charitable persons who so liberally contributed towards the expenses of the poorhouses in the Kadi division, or worked honorarily in connection with them, and their special donations and amounts, have not yet all been received. But in connection with the poorhouses at Patan, Javeri Chaganlal Maganlal, Shet Karamchand Motichand of Kota, Shet Lalubhai Nathubhai, Javeri Ameechand Panalal, and Shet Kilabhai Devchand are known to have liberally contributed towards the funds. Shet Karamchand Motichand maintained, in addition, a poorhouse of his own. In the same manner Soni Hari Walabh Gulabchand and the widow of the late Govardhan Manchand also maintained small poorhouses. The efforts of Dr. Balabhai Maganlal were specially instrumental in bringing together large collections in Patan. He himself being a Jain and highly popular, was greatly respected in the community, and wealthy Jain bankers and merchants gave a willing ear to his advice. His personal exertions in looking after the physical welfare of the people, though undertaken in the discharge of his duties, deserve more than passing mention. In connection with a poorhouse at Visnagar the names of Rav Bahadur Purshotam Vrijrai and Shet Suraj Mal Leherchand, trustees of the late Majmundar Shivashankar Shobharam, stand prominently out, by reason of the liberal contributions they made to the institution from the estates of the deceased. For the maintenance of the Mahajan poorhouse at Visnagar, Shet Suraj Mal Leherchand, Mansukhbhai Salubhai, Jamnadas Gokaldas, Gokalbhai Mulchand, Gokalbhai Dawlatram, and Mathurbhai Mulchand assisted by liberal contributions. Shet Gokalbhai Dawlatram, in addition to his liberal donations, managed to maintain a poorhouse of his own. The widow of the late Parikha Vrijlal Baldev also maintained another. At Vadnagar, the Mahajan poorhouse was started and maintained through the special efforts of Shets Manibhai Revadas, Mohanlal, and Fatechand, who themselves made large gifts and induced others to contribute. At Sidhpur the charities of the Mullaji, preceptor of the Vohora community, and of Shet Allibhai and Shet Usafali are known. The Mehsana poorhouse owed its existence to the efforts of Shet Virchand Jadavji.

Other Divisions.—The three poorhouses started in the Navsari division, and specially the one at Kathore, which managed to relieve the largest number in that division, reflect great credit upon the public spirit of their organisers, amongst whom the name of Mr. Bhimbhai Himatram may be prominently mentioned. In the Amreli division the Subha brings to notice the charities of Shet Keshavlal Tribhovandas of Damnagar, who managed to give relief to a large number of people in various ways. The relief of 1,346,450 units in the Baroda division could not have been secured without special endeavours on the part of the Subha.

Amreli Private Charities.—The Mahajans of Amreli collected Rs. 3000 for cheap-grain shops and gratuitous relief to the poor. They also supplied clothes to the indigent, and collected Rs. 2000 for providing fodder for the cattle. The owners of the ginning factories and two other Shetias supplied cooked bread daily to the poor, the total expenditure coming to about Rs. 1000. The officials and Mahajans of Kodinar collected about Rs. 300 and used the sum in giving cooked food to the poor; while Sardar Umar Jamal sent 215 maunds of rice from Bombay for the poor. The charities in the Damnagar and Okhamandal Talukas, being more extensive, are separately mentioned.

Damnagar Taluka.—Shet Keshavlal Tribhovandas has done most for the Taluka, and his charity stands pre-eminently remarkable. In September, October, and November he sold corn at cheap rates to the needy. Poor people from a distance of 25 miles are reported to have taken advantage of the shop; and from 2000 to 5000 persons are reported to have daily made purchases there for some time. All the year round he prudently managed to keep down the price of corn in the bazar by selling at moderate rates to all comers. For this purpose he had collected a very large store of corn by purchases made in Bombay and elsewhere. He also maintained a few people gratuitously for six months, and 64 orphans for two months. In an asylum for cattle he spent over Rs. 10,000. He gave employment to many labourers in conveying from the Dhassa station to Damnagar the large stores of grain he had purchased, while others again found work in the storehouses. Shet Damodar Jagjivan distributed cooked bread once a day (½ a seer to each person) from December 1899, at an expenditure of Rs. 150 per month. Daudbhai Modabhai, Girasia of Rupavati, though himself in anything but a flourishing condition, spent over Rs. 1000 in purchasing and preserving cattle.

Dwarka and Beyt Charities.—It need not be said that the religiously-inclined Hindus of Bombay and other places were forward in the relief of men and cattle in these towns, so sacred in their estimation. Thakar Purshotam Visram Mavji of Verwala alone spent a sum of Rs. 17,683 in opening a cheap grain shop. Thakar Kalidas Jutha devoted Rs.3700 towards clothes and food for men and grass for cattle. Shet Mulji Dharamsi gave Rs. 750 for a cheap-grain shop; and Shet Narandas Hemraj contributed Rs. 1000 for the same purpose. The large sum of Rs. 41,848 was privately spent in Sadavarats (gratuitous corn or food) to pilgrims and others in Dwarka Verwala, Gopi, Kuranga, and Amliara. The charities in Beyt are given below:—

	Rs.
From the temples	3,500
Shets Jeram and Abji Shivji of Kach Mundra	11,000
Raja Pratapsingji of Jambu	1,100
Luvana Topan Sundarji of Kach . . .	880
Thakar Keshowji Ravji of Bombay . .	2,750
" Ramdas Bhanji of Verwala . .	1,650
" Jadavji Tulsidas of Beyt . . .	2,200
" Vaghji Corejee of Kach Tora . .	1,375
" Laxmidas Ladha of Kach Mundra .	1,650
" Anandji Visram of Kach Mandvi .	1,925
" Purshotam Visram Mavji of Bombay	2,053
" Ratansi Mulji of Bombay . . .	1,300
" Chatrabhuj Morarji	725
Bombay Mahajans	1,070
Bombay market traders of Okha . . .	1,595
Smaller items	2,927
Total Rs.	37,700

Navsari Private Charities.—Subscriptions to the amount of Rs. 7530 were collected by Mr. Maneklal Vakil and Mr. Navroji Tamboli, for a cheap-grain shop, which involved an expenditure of Rs. 7300. Mr. Ibrahim Suleman opened a cheap-grain shop in Kathore, and Mr. Ismal Ahmed in Variav; but the amounts spent by them are not forthcoming.

Kadi Private Charities.—The Mahajans of Patan, under the advice of their leaders, Shets Hirachand Khemchand and Jiva Virchand, opened a cheap-grain shop and continued it for some months. The pressure on the shop was always heavy; and the amount of loss is estimated at Rs. 18,000. A smaller shop started by the Sodagars of Patan under Mian Ali Ibraham had about Rs. 300 spent upon it. The only other shop in the division was opened by the Mahajans at Vijapur; it cost them about Rs. 462. The officers and other Government servants of the division, under the leadership of the Subha, for the most part contributed half a month's salary each to a fund in aid of the Zenana and Parda women and respectable people, to supply them with money and clothes, and to convey help to the inmates of the private poorhouses. Rs. 4272 were subscribed and Rs. 1150 expended up to the end of the year.

Management of Baroda Poorhouses.—Thanks are due to Ramji Santuji Avte, editor of the Baroda *Vatchal*, and Mr. Dharnidhar Balvant Vakanker for the untiring energy with which they worked in their disinterested management of the station (Rode's Dharmshalla) and the Daliavadi poorhouses, which were models of order, cleanliness, and organisation.

III.—Concluding Remarks

. . . . .

His Excellency the Dewan.—It does not behove a subordinate officer to speak of the work of his superiors, but it may not be deemed out of place or over-bold in me to say one word as to how His Excellency the Dewan Saheb guided all the departments under him. Every officer knows how ready he was, at any time of the day, to help and advise, to instruct and order. His information was marvellous, and it is therefore no wonder that his directions were implicitly obeyed.

His Highness's Secretaries.—Mr. Usafali Jamadar, B.A., barrister at law, and Mr. Manubhai N. Mehta, M.A., LL.B., Secretaries to His Highness the Maharaja Saheb, had no light-work to perform . . . in explaining the tippans, writing out Huzur orders, making special inquiries, revelling in a study of their subject. Their assiduity and readiness deserve every praise.

The Famine Officers.—The head of the Revenue and Famine Departments, Mr. Ramchandra V. Dhamnaskar, did not spare himself in the tours of inspection, which enabled him to propose many useful suggestions for relief; he also accompanied His Highness in some of his tours. The most difficult points of administration were discussed by him personally both with His Highness and His Excellency, and the Famine Office always relied with confidence on his tact and advice. On Mr. Graham R. Lynn, the Chief Engineer, devolved the responsible duty, as head of the Public Works Department, of seeing that all the works that were needed for relief were promptly submitted, with estimates and plans, where possible, and of ordering and looking to their proper execution, when once they had been sanctioned. It was due to his familiarity with all parts of the districts and his high professional attainments that so many works were kept running at the same time. The Executive Engineers and the other officers of the Department carried out his orders to the best of their ability. On the Subhas of the divisions devolved the onerous work of looking to every detail of relief for their divisions. They all came up to the emergency. Each might have had his own views in regard to the best way of affording relief; but all were inspired with the laudable zeal of doing all that could be done for their divisions. Mr. Samarth justly takes credit to himself for keeping all his men in hand in Amreli and not allowing them to deteriorate or any one to die of want, till the epidemic of cholera upset his schemes. Mr. Vanekar was most successful in appealing to the co-operation of the wealthy people of the Kadi division, and in starting and maintaining poorhouses, which, owing partly to the ready help given by Dr. Balabhai, were models of order and cleanliness. Mr. Khaserao Jadhav was, as usual, most popular with the people of Baroda. His demands for money were irrepressible, but his supervision was strict and intolerant of deceptions. To him the State is indebted for the conception of many engineering projects, particularly irrigational ones. Mr. Kershaw was always brimful of sympathy for the poor of his Navsari division, and did much for the relief of the Forest tribes. The heads of the Medical and Police Departments carried out all the Huzur orders and the provisions of the code smoothly and carefully. It need not be said that, working as they were under the direct orders of the Maharaja, all officers of all departments and grades were animated with the desire to do their duty loyally and efficiently. Every one worked to the best of his judgment with single-minded zeal and energy, and with such harmony that there was hardly any disagreement in the joint working of the different departments.

It is natural that no mention should have been made here of the work performed by the Famine Commissioner. His Highness looked constantly and minutely into his work, and it must be left to him to say how it was done. But prominent notice may, at any rate, be taken of the work of the Famine Assistants, Mr. Ramchandra Abaji Raje and Mr. Manchharam Bhagvanji, who never flagged in their zeal and labour under such heavy pressure of work as few could have borne. Great injustice would be done to these deserving servants if their valuable services did not receive the fullest acknowledgment. The previous assistant, Mr. Ravji B. Patel, who is intelligent and resourceful, also did good service.

The name of Mr. Rustamji R. Kothawala, who rendered most valuable service in the Kadi division, first as the officer superintending the administration and use of tagavi for wells, and then as assistant to the Subha, must also be added. He is an expert in revenue matters, and his services were deservedly applauded.

Mr. D. T. Pavri, Mr. R. N. Ambegavkur, and Mr. Appa Saheb Mohite also rendered useful service in the matter of new wells.

THE END